SOUNDS
LIKE ME

My Life (so far) in Song

SARA BAREILLES

SIMON & SCHUSTER PAPERBACKS

New York London Toronto Sydney New Delhi

Simon & Schuster Paperbacks
An Imprint of Simon & Schuster, Inc.
1230 Avenue of the Americas
New York, NY 10020

Copyright © 2015 by Sara Bareilles

Unless otherwise noted, all photographs are part of the author's collection.

All rights reserved, including the right to reproduce this book or portions thereof in any form whatsoever. For information address Simon & Schuster Paperbacks Subsidiary Rights Department, 1230 Avenue of the Americas, New York, NY 10020.

First Simon & Schuster trade paperback edition October 2019

SIMON & SCHUSTER PAPERBACKS and colophon are registered trademarks of Simon & Schuster, Inc.

For information about special discounts for bulk purchases, please contact Simon & Schuster Special Sales at 1-866-506-1949 or business@simonandschuster.com.

The Simon & Schuster Speakers Bureau can bring authors to your live event. For more information or to book an event contact the Simon & Schuster Speakers Bureau at 1-866-248-3049 or visit our website at www.simonspeakers.com.

Interior design by Laura Palese

Manufactured in the United States of America

3 5 7 9 10 8 6 4

The Library of Congress has cataloged the hardcover edition as follows:
Bareilles, Sara.
Sounds like me : my life (so far) in song / Sara Bareilles.—First Simon & Schuster hardcover edition.
pages cm
1. Bareilles, Sara. 2. Singers—United States—Biography. I. Title.
ML420.B166A3 2015
782.42164092—dc23
[B]
2015015754

ISBN 978-1-4767-2777-6
ISBN 978-1-9821-4222-3 (pbk)
ISBN 978-1-4767-2778-3 (ebook)

———

This book is for three blazing and fierce
young fires, Abby, Megan, and Melody. May
you be brave and wild and search for *your*
sound in this beautiful world, knowing you are
already perfect, and endlessly loved.

———

CONTENTS

FOREWORD

BY BEN FOLDS

MY INTRODUCTION TO SARA was seeing her face on the free promotional CD of her major label debut *Little Voice* before using it to prop up an uneven leg of my entertainment center in the corner of my living room. I'm pretty sure I didn't even take it out of the clear wrapper, as I already had an opener for my next tour. I could hear the crunch of the plastic case as the shelf settled into a satisfactory approximation of level. I was glad I got that in the mail! A few months later, when I heard Love Song in a shoe store, I was ashamed. I walked across the mall parking lot to Best Buy to buy a copy sans hole in singer's face. It deserved to be purchased and played to death, and so it was.

Years later, Sara Bareilles is one of my favorite humans in the world, and in my opinion, one of the finest singers and pop music artists of our time. I can tell you firsthand that whether it's having a laugh stageside before a performance, a minor breakdown at a coffee shop during recording sessions, or attempting to escape the Sony Studios parking lot to avoid more reality TV hair extensions, Sara is the same Sara who you hear on your iPod, on the radio, or while buying shoes. She will soon be keeping you company for the next two hundred pages in that same brilliant voice that has won her a mainstream audience that follows her every word with the zeal of a small cult. For me, this book, like her songs, is like having a conversation with the lady herself, minus my constant interruptions. In this case, that bit is nicely contained in this single-page foreword that you can skip if you like, that in fact could have been boiled down to this:

Dear Sara,

Please forgive me for the hole I put in your face and for allowing TV producers to dress you in twenty-inch high-heeled stilettos. You are a true friend, a brilliant musical theater composer, and now a damn book author. You constantly uphold my faith in people, music, and still, after all these years, the corner of my entertainment center.

You are beautiful.

Ben

AN INTRODUCTION

——

I **HAVE BEEN WRITING** this book for over two years.

Over two years for eight essays.

Over two years for eight essays about myself, whom I spend a great deal of time with, and know a lot about. If you're not great with subtext, I'll help you out:

Writing this book was difficult.

I said yes to this project back in 2013, because I loved the *idea* of writing a book. That's like buying white jeans because you like the *idea* of looking good in them. I think we all know where this is headed. It was nice at first. I smugly skated around on the phrase, "I'm working on a book right now. . . ." and people gave me raised eyebrows and looks of wonderment and I felt like sparkly peppermint candy for a few months. Then the edges faded and shit got real. Instead of a cabin in the woods with a typewriter and a basset hound, I had a laptop, a winter in New York, a deadline, and anxiety.

I kicked and screamed and wrestled and lost. I traveled and ignored and distracted and apologized. I watched it like a rattlesnake out of the corner of my eye and hoped it would just slither away. When it didn't, I spent countless hours in coffee shops, restaurants, and at my kitchen table, writing to meet a "hard" deadline that came and went well over a year ago. I considered giving back the money I got from the publisher. I considered putting this off for another few years until I became smart enough or wise enough or funny enough to know how to do this. Then, at the encouragement of my managers, I decided to take a long break from it.

I wrote a musical.

It was easier to *write a musical* than this set of eight essays.

After about a year and a half of fighting it, I finally surrendered. I took a break from flogging myself with the question, "What business do I have writing a book?" and decided to do it anyway. That question didn't have an answer, and the truth is that nobody out there in the world *needs* this book. Nobody but me. I needed it.

It taught me to love something difficult.

Writing this book *was* hard. In fact, I would say it's the hardest thing I've ever done. But the epiphany was recognizing that I could maybe still love this thing not only in spite of it being challenging, but *because* of it. It was as I sat with that truth that I understood why I fought this so hard. It feels infinitely more vulnerable to speak about my life without the metaphor and mask of music or my singing voice. I had to take a look at who I am without those things. These essays are a much more direct line to the inner workings of my mind and my heart, and that's an exposed place to find yourself and your little machine.

I leaned on the familiar foundation of my own music to find my way into this new kind of writing, and eventually the book evolved into a collection of stories, each anchored by a song. It felt right to weave my music into this writing in some way, and it helped the essays start flowing like the tiny belabored trickle they were intended to be. I tried to be candid. I tried to be honest. I tried to remember things in an unbiased way. I tried to be at least a little funny. I tried not to gossip. I tried to be myself, as wholeheartedly as possible. I started to enjoy it, and that was astonishing. I neared the finish line bruised but happy, all the while dodging the main question anyone would ask. . . .

Deciding what to call this book almost drove me crazy. In a very formal meeting surrounded by a team of literary professionals, my publisher asked me casually, "So have you thought at all about a title?" He smiled. I fake-smiled. He had no idea how much time I had already spent wildly scraping my insides for this oh-so-elusive set of words. Hours and days and weeks making lists of possible titles, some of which still speak beautifully to the emotional state I was in along the way. . . .

Wait, So I'm in Charge?
Trying Too Hard
Being a Person Is Really Hard
I'm Not Going to Write You a Book
I Don't Feel Like Being Funny
Utterly Uncool
Whatever It Is, It's Not What You're Thinking

I spared him my knee-jerk reaction of leaping across the table and fighting him like a feral cat, and instead told him I was "working on it."

I was on my eighth and final essay, sitting at my kitchen table looking out my window at the never-ending winter of New York, and thinking for the millionth time about what I wanted to call the book. I thought about the approach I was taking with the essays. About how the essays felt like they reflected my life on a larger scale. I wanted them to be honest. I wanted them to be authentic. I wanted to make sure that when I read them back, they sounded like me (*cue light bulb).

So here we are.

This book is some of my story and some of my songs.

It was a labor of avoidance, then hate, then love, and I'm glad I stayed around long enough to witness the transformation.

I wrote it for you.

It sounds like me.

ONCE
UPON
another
TIME

CHAPTER
one

Once Upon Another time

Once upon another time
Somebody's hands who felt like mine
Turned the key and took a drive
Was free.
The highway curved, the sun sank low
♥ BUCKLEY on the radio
cigarette was burning slow
So breathe
        Just yellow lines and tire marks
And sun-kissed skin and handlebars
And where I stood was where I was to be
    No ~~enemies~~ Enemies to call my own
    No porch light on to pull me home
        And where I was is beautiful
                    Because
                    I
                    was
                    free.
Once upon Another time
    Before I knew which life was mine
    Before I left the child behind me
    I saw myself in summer nights
    And stars lit up like candlelight
        I made my wish but mostly
            I believed...

ONCE UPON ANOTHER TIME

AS A CHILD I was a tomboy, and felt most myself with my clothes and my hands dirty, running through the woods with my two dogs by my side, following the clues of a self-laid treasure hunt, or clip-clopping along on my make-believe pony through a soft bed of pine needles. Our house was on five acres of redwood forest, and I spent the vast majority of my kid days out in what felt like cavernous wilderness. I wrote one of my first songs in my backyard, but realize now that it's maybe more creepy than cute to sing a song called My Special Place.

/ *My dad's house in Eureka*

*My cousin Christy and I at my uncle's house
(just up the hill from my house)*

My uncle and his family lived next door to us, separated
by an acre of field and forest. We were lucky to be close to
our extended family, and the organized chaos of our combined
houses is the backdrop for some of my best memories. Their
house mirrored our own home down the hill: a sizable but mod-
est ranch-style redwood house, tucked under the trees, where
most things are a little bit broken but that's okay. There were
always tons of people, some colorfully exaggerated stories

being told around a table, plenty to eat, and a roaring fire in the fireplace.

I have fifteen first cousins on my dad's side, seven of whom grew up alongside my sisters and me. We all loved playing together, and this meant that any family gathering brought with it a barrage of wrestling matches and races and yelling and "Where is your sister!?" and hide-and-seek and card games and skits. There was crying and laughing and everything in between. Five of my cousins are adopted and, as a multiracial family, we kids looked like a United Colors of Benetton ad, but instead of Benetton our family was advertising Ross Dress for Less and Goodwill. It was awesome.

I was closest to my cousin Christy, who is two years older than me. She stood almost a foot taller than me, with caramel skin and a bright, toothy smile. Many of my most idyllic childhood moments involved her.

Summers were my favorite, of course. I couldn't wait for that succession of days that felt absolutely endless when we could gorge ourselves on our own imaginations. Once, we built an enormous haystack out of the cut grasses in the field and spent the afternoon burrowing a hole from one side to the other, leaving a tunnel high enough to sit cross-legged in. At the time, I figured we would probably move some stuff in and live out the rest of the summer there, but then we got hungry and *Full House* was on. We climbed woodpiles where I caught a splinter between my butt cheeks and had to lie on my stomach until my mom came to help. We roamed the creek and caught frogs and made them tiny furniture that they hardly ever used or appreciated. Those same kinds of frogs serenaded us on the many nights we slept outside on Christy's back deck in sleeping bags, under the canopy of thick branches. Overnight, the tree limbs would become saturated with the coastal fog's moisture, and by morning, we'd be soaked with dew. We "swam" in swampy, muddy holes that had been dug for planting trees, and made a game of trying to get our legs (in our fathers' rubber boots) stuck in the mud. Our favorite spot to end up was "The Tree," a network of knotty, gnarled branches that dangled over a tiny creek, complete with a rope swing. We'd lie back and talk endlessly about things I can't remember even a little now.

When we both got horses around the same time, my little-girl brain almost exploded.

Too.

Much.

Joy.

To.

Compute.

Christy was the first to get her horse, when she was around fifteen. Lady was a tall, lean chestnut mare, and I ached with envy. I pestered and whined until my dad eventually caved in and we got Shiloh, a little Welsh pony and Arabian mix who I loved even more than I loved Lady. Shiloh was the same color as redwood tree bark, with a regal face and a stout little body. And even at his relatively ripe old age of sixteen, he had way more energy than I could handle. He was a retired barrel-racing horse and, among many things, taught me that I hate barrel racing.

The sweet family that sold us Shiloh was involved in the local rodeos. They were true horse people: they owned enormous trucks with extra wheels, went trail riding on weekends, and wore cowboy hats and big belt buckles unironically. They were like freaking superheroes. They were also very encouraging of my decision to enter the barrel-racing event at an upcoming rodeo, even though I had never even tried it before. Shiloh was an old pro, and how hard could it be?

For those of you unfamiliar with barrel racing: a buzzer rings and a rider hangs on for dear life as a horse shoots off like a bat out of hell toward some big empty oil barrels placed strategically at one end of an arena and runs around them as fast as he can and then races back to the other end of the arena completely of his own free will while the rider tries not to fall off or cry because she thinks she broke her vagina and thank God the horse finally stopped and is that my pee? It's really fun.

I only participated in that one rodeo.

I was the baby of my family, with two older sisters and six and nine years separating us. Because of our age difference, we didn't have much in common, and I hated that more than anything. In grade school, I was dying to hang out with my sisters and their friends. I wanted everybody to play with My Little Pony castles and make fart jokes with me, but they only wanted to wear pastel colors and watch *The Breakfast Club*. It was devastating. My two sisters shared clothes and friends and secrets with each other, and I longed to be a part of that connection, but I was still just too young. (To all the frustrated little siblings out there: hold tight. This all changes when you get older.)

My oldest sister, Stacey, kind and sensitive, always had super-cute boyfriends and was involved with school and sports, but I mostly vividly remember her interest in music, especially musical theater. Indulging my craving to be included in anything performance related, she taught me a dance routine to Janet Jackson's Nasty Boys (which is a questionable choice now that I think about it, Stace). I gleefully danced alongside her in front of the big picture window we used as a mirror. She is a terrifically talented singer and actress, and did all kinds of performances all through high school and college. This is a huge part of why I ever imagined myself being onstage in the first place. Sometimes it's easier to imagine yourself somewhere somebody's already been. She was my musical idol and encouraged me by singing with me. She was also my very first cowriter. We wrote a song together when I was probably five or six, called I Love a Parade.

The lyrics were:

I love a parade.

And I won't be afraid.

(After that we just sang "oooooooh.")

Our middle sister, Jenny, has a kind of magnetism within our family, and it's not an uncommon occurrence that over a beer she has somehow heard your deepest, darkest secrets without even asking. She is blessed with an innate ability to make people feel seen, heard, and safe, meanwhile keeping her own vulnerability tucked just beneath the surface of her own skin. She shares it with only a very select and privileged few. An expertly animated storyteller, she is funny as hell, as well as a very gifted actress. I remember watching her in a play called *A Bad Year for Tomatoes* when she was in high school, where she donned a gray wig and oversize glasses. I almost peed my pants watching her race around the stage in a muumuu, acting outrageous and talking with a lisp. She always knew how to get a laugh. And, according to my Grandma, "She's *very* good at basketball."

In spite of our age difference, they were endlessly sweet to me, and I have wonderful memories of being with my sisters. My favorite ones, though, are connected to music. We didn't grow up listening to a lot of music all together. Given the sheer number of people shuffling through the house at any given time, there was usually so much commotion from various sports and activities and theater events that music became an afterthought. Christmas, however, was an exception. The whole season was filled with music, be it church hymns or the Jackson 5 Christmas album. I *loved* it. I always looked forward to Michael's tiny, perfect voice zipping up and down from the rafters singing I Saw Mommy Kissing Santa Claus as the entire family sifted through the hundreds of delicate ornaments tucked away in shoe boxes and decided how to ration them among the tree branches. Everyone sang along, and I felt like we were *finally* becoming more like the Von Trapps, just like I had been praying for.

The absolute best, best, best times for me were singing and performing little skits with Jenny and Stacey on the hearth of our fireplace in front of Mom and Dad and our extended family. We would alternate between impromptu choreography, three-part harmony on Amazing Grace, Sweeney Sisters medleys, and Sonny and Cher impersonations. I would laugh until my sides hurt and I didn't really care what we were doing just so long as I got to do it with them. That statement holds true for me today.

My dad juggled an insurance-adjusting business with part-time logging and was always racing around, busy with something. To this day, he loves working outside more than anything, and he taught me how to use a wood splitter, how to drive a Caterpillar, and what a truly happy man is. My mom was our devoted community organizer. In addition to part-time work, she helped run every school function and fund-raiser that came her way when we were young and, as we got older, hosted every birthday and every cast party for her friends in our community theater. She taught me the genius of the *Golden Girls*, how to make berry pie, the importance of thank-you notes, and the art of making someone else feel special. My parents were consummate hosts, and our home was the seat of endless parties and holiday gatherings filled with their friends, our enormous extended family, and anyone who might otherwise be eating Thanksgiving dinner alone. My uncle's house up the hill operated in the same way, and collectively they all taught us generosity, kindness, and inclusion, and that you always share what you have, even when it's not much. My parents managed to construct a little safe haven for my sisters and me to build ourselves within, which seems almost impossible to me when I think about how quickly childhood seems to disappear these days. They have taught me about the truest kind of love: the kind that is steadfast and strong, even when it changes shape.

My family at Easter circa 1985

My folks divorced when I was twelve. I have a vague memory of my mom calling me in from playing outside in the field one afternoon because we needed to have a talk. Time slowed down and my brain's little wheels were turning very, very slowly, trying to make sense of what Mom was saying. *We love each other very much, but things are going to change. Mom is going to go live somewhere else. We both still love you very much and it's not your fault.*

It was like a foreign language I couldn't interpret.

The next couple of weeks were a fog that included my sister Jenny driving off to her freshman year of college, six hours away, and my mom driving her little gray Toyota Cressida to a tiny yellow house with a big oak tree in the front yard, about a mile and a half from what had been our family home. That mile and a half might as well have been a light-year.

I was devastated but tried not to show it. Mom and Dad were both so sad already, and verbal communication wasn't our family's strong suit. I don't think I fully understood what I was feeling anyway. Anger. Disappointment. Confusion. Grief. Helplessness. With my sisters both gone to college, I was the only child left in the house to divide up my stuff and decide whether I would keep my Kirk Cameron poster and my Caboodle at my mom or my dad's house. I didn't want there to *be* a "Mom's house," much less surrender some of my things to take over there. In the end, I chose my shittiest stuff to take to my mom's, a tiny rebellion against the separation. My Caboodle and my Bart Simpson jean jacket stayed at Dad's.

My emotional world imploded, and there is nothing that could have been said or done to make it easier. No one was in the wrong, and maybe that is what made it so painful. I wanted someone to blame, but instead got the two people I loved most doing their best to navigate uncharted waters. Not knowing how to talk about it, I went inward with my sadness and started writing in journals more often. This would become an important part of my adolescence, and my developing understanding of myself. It tided me over while time did what it always does: softened the hard edges.

Eventually my parents blazed a pretty remarkable trail toward lives that now orbit each other in a beautiful way. Fast-forward to the present day, and my parents and step-parents are all the best of friends. (True!) We all take trips together. We share every major holiday and then some. They hang out even when us kids aren't in town. They make dinner for each other and play cards and drink wine and want each other to be happy. We all dance to Love Shack by the B-52s at every family gathering, which I think is really the most important part.

It was a long road getting there, but over the years we have redefined the word *family* to encompass all iterations of our pasts. For Christmas this year, my dad, Paul, and my stepdad, Ron, got matching shirts from my little sister Melody, a precious, perfect gift of a girl who came after my dad and Betsy married. One of the shirts says RON'S MY BUDDY, and the other says PAUL'S MY BUDDY. Dad wore his shirt to Christmas dinner.

The whole thing is "pretty neat," as my dad would say.

It's unpredictable how we are changed by what challenges us as children. For example, dealing with the divorce was difficult but inadvertently encouraged me to go to my private journals and write. But that wasn't the hardest part of my childhood. My greatest struggle is a big part of why I stand onstage.

I sing because I was a fat kid.

I use the term *fat kid* to describe my experience as a child, because that is the label I was given by my peers, and at the time, that equated to feeling different and somehow bad. But I don't see my former self that same way now. *Fat* means

St. Bernard's Elementary classroom photo, 1988

nothing. It is a three-letter word that, when you break it down, refers to the thing in food that makes it taste good, so I love fat. (Hey bacon, call me. ;-)) And as an adjective, the word is completely subjective. I see it get abused and misused all the time. I see magazines wrap it around strong, healthy bodies in ridicule. I see beautiful women among my friends and family do the same thing. One in particular, in my mirror, does it all the time. I have learned to hate that word because it was used as a cruel, incendiary insult in my own life, but I wish I could change my relationship with it. I wish I could go back in time and deconstruct the power that it had.

Maybe that's what I'm doing now.

My dysfunctional relationship with my body started around third grade, sparked by comments from a small group of boys at my Catholic school whom I considered my friends. I felt surprised by it when it first started happening. Like, I didn't know I was fat. In my mind, there hadn't really been anything wrong with me, until they told me there was. And even then I didn't really know what to do about it. Now, when I look at pictures of myself at that age, I know there was absolutely nothing "wrong" with me at all, but some thoughtless words carved out a story that I believed, and my body obsession began.

In the few years that followed, I became increasingly self-critical. I fixated on counting my stomach rolls and paying attention to whether or not my thighs rubbed together when I walked. I hated my knees and the way they interrupted the line of my legs, so I never ever wore shorts. (Side note: I also never wore sandals because of a foot fungus. One of the many unsuccessful ways we tried treating it was soaking my foot in some weird crystals that turned it purple.) I secretly compared the size of my chubby little hands to those of the other little girls in my classes and came to the conclusion that it was really my knuckles that were the problem, and if I just had smaller knuckles everything would be fine. My personality got bigger and bigger among my peers to distract them from my body, and I acted more and more like a clown to fill the space that had otherwise been filled with insults. My eating habits didn't help either; regularly devouring Cup Noodles two at a time as an after-school snack, or my own invention . . . crouton cereal. (Sourdough croutons in a bowl, drenched with Italian dressing. Still delicious.) Food was a frenemy, making me feel better and worse at the same time. My "mean girls" were Lay's potato chips and salami.

The summer before seventh grade I made a concerted effort to change. I started jogging through my neighborhood and came home red-faced and sick to my stomach. I did sit-ups. I ate more salads and less cake, and once I was away from the constant feedback loop of my classmates' chatter, I started to feel pretty good about myself. I felt stronger, the jogging started getting easier, and although the changes were slight, on the first day of school I looked in the mirror in my school uniform and felt content.

I was disappointed when no one at school noticed my phoenix-like rise out of my own fat ashes that first day, but I decided they would certainly notice soon enough. During recess in that first week back, I played basketball with a few of the boys. In a friendly tussle with me over possession of the ball, one of them called me a "tub o' lard" and snatched the ball from my stunned, normal-size knuckles. I pretended not to notice because I didn't want him to know how biting those words were. Or how much time and energy I had spent trying to shed that image, and how much it leveled me that all my hard work hadn't changed anything. It was crushing to realize that my identity among them had been branded upon me, and that there was really no changing it. I finished the game and then cried in private that day because I thought the only thing worse than being hurt was letting it be seen by the person who hurt me.

You don't ever completely shed those feelings. Those images of myself swim inside me even now, and it's disturbing how much pleasure I still feel ripple through me when I share this part of my story and someone says they can't see it—that they can't imagine me as a fat kid. I see her every single day. As recently as a few months ago, I left a dance class because I couldn't stand the way I looked in the mirror at the front of the room. I'm not proud of that, and I don't succumb to those old stories as often as I used to, but it feels like the most defining characteristic of my life. It trumps that I was a tomboy, or that I was loved, or that I was goofy, or that I was an animal lover. It is my involuntary tattoo.

I transferred schools at the end of that year. My mom helped me make that decision. She has always been an exceptionally comforting person when it really counts, and has a way of making you feel unconditionally perfect even though we both know it's just a smoke screen. No one is perfect, but it's also nice to sometimes just believe her. It must have been hard for her to see her daughter so upset so many times after school. I cried to her and complained and wailed and blamed the other kids incessantly. One day she took a new approach with me, and instead of being comforting and soft, she was exasperated and laid it all out on the line.

"You can't just keep complaining about it! What do you want to do, Sara? Do you want to change schools or not?!"

It felt like a slap in the face, but in a good way. I took her advice, and I'm so glad. Public school offered me a clean slate and an opportunity to shed my Catholic-school skin and reemerge as one of the best things we can ever be: nobody.

No one knew me. No one cared. It was amazing. I got to reinvent myself in flannel shirts and '90s boot-cut jeans, constructing a new self-image while the kids in my new school had no idea I was shedding anything. My brand-new set of friends didn't seem to care about or notice my body at all, and although I was still obsessing internally, I wasn't tortured by my circumstances anymore. I tried new things. I got involved with sports and extracurricular activities and was surprised at how quickly I formed new and meaningful friendships. While my girlfriends and I were deciding which boys we were crushing on (Mike Rios, I still love you!!!), they also discovered that I could sing. My voice became a deep source of pride for me, and gained me admiration from my new peers. My extroverted personality was growing, and I loved getting attention for something positive for a change. Singing became a part of my social identity, which was something that would stay with

Playing Fern in a local theater
production of Charlotte's Web, *1993*

me for a very long time. This feeling went hand in hand with another new world that was simultaneously unfolding, asking to be explored.

*The day of my seventh-grade
graduation, at home playing piano*

The theater.

My mom and sisters had been involved in theater productions for as long as I can remember, and some of my most floaty,
blissful moments as a kid were among their theater friends.
Loud, brash, eccentric, creative, accepting, and hilarious, they
represented a spectrum of people I could see myself inside of.
Their bright passion for being in the spotlight was something
I could relate to, and maybe it was possible for me as well.
Among these people, I never felt fat. I never felt ugly. I was
welcomed into the center of all of it. The cast parties were (of
course) hosted by my mom, and dancing and singing at the top
of my lungs to our beloved Love Shack, I felt truly happy. This
was a community of people who made me feel accepted and
celebrated, and I wanted more of that.

Singing. Music. Performance. Those things had been
threaded through my whole childhood. Whether it was our
mini variety shows on the fireplace hearth, or singing along
to my dad playing the piano late at night with a little glass of
red wine (he had the wine, I had that bowl of croutons), I had
always been a natural singer. I had a good ear, and although
the mechanics of playing along to myself on the piano were
much more difficult, I always had an affinity for it. I took piano
lessons for a little while in the second grade, but as soon as my
piano teacher (who pronounced my name "SAY-rah") asked
me to do something different with my left hand than my right
hand, I was overwhelmed and over it. But my love of music
and of the piano in particular stayed. And now, I was seeing
performance in a whole new light. My mom, my sisters, and

their friends sparkled onstage in dozens of community theater productions. When Stacey was Eva Perón in *Evita*, I must have seen it seven or eight times. It was intoxicating. The drama, the costume, the emotion, the lights, the attention, the company of actors. I couldn't wait to get the chance to officially be a part of an artistic community.

I got cast in my first show alongside my sister Stacey when I was around thirteen. The experience was an awakening for me. I wore a shin-length gingham dress and pigtail braids, and played a little girl living on the prairie in a show called *Quilters*. I sang a solo about rolling green hills, and preparing for that moment, when all eyes were on me, was my favorite part of the show. I could feel the weight of being handed the attention of an audience and somehow knew how to hold that space, probably from watching my family before me. I felt powerful. And strong. And important. And beautiful. I was hooked. I wanted more and more of that feeling and I sought it out. Over the next few years, I had supporting roles in community theater productions of *The Mystery of Edwin Drood* and *Charlotte's Web*. When I got the lead in *Little Shop of Horrors* at my high school, I was in heaven. I sang in all sorts of choirs and musical ensembles and was not only welcomed into that world, but validated and rewarded. I sang Cyndi Lauper's Time After Time at our high school graduation, and watched my friends get emotional. It made me feel like I added something of value to the experience, and I was proud of that. I started writing music, and though I didn't yet share it, I had found my place by finding my voice.

I still spend a lot of time inside the rose-colored and complicated nostalgia of childhood. I still see myself as a little girl a lot of the time. Those years were precious as well as painful, and they taught me a lot. I learned empathy. I learned humor. I learned compassion. I learned how to soothe myself with my own private world of writing. In the midst of a group of peers who only made room for me sometimes, I sought out the places where I felt acceptance. I found it first in nature, and then on the stage, through performance. We go toward the softest places to land, and sometimes they are few and far between. I was lucky to find some sort of path that stretched out in front of me, like yellow lines on a freeway, and even luckier to have the feeling that it was going to take me somewhere special.

GRAVITY

CHAPTER
two

Gravity

Something always brings me back to you
It never takes too long
No matter what I say or do
I'll still feel you here, till The moment
  I'm gone
You hold me without touch
  You keep me without chains
I never wanted anything so much
Than to drown in your love and not feel
  your rain.

Set me free,
    leave me be
I don't want to fall another moment
  into your gravity
Here I am, and I stand so tall

  I'm just the way I'm supposed to be
    But you're on to me
        And all over me
You loved me cause I'm fragile
    when I Thought That I was strong
But you touch me for a little while
      And all my fragile strength is gone
Set me free leave me be
    I don't want to fall another moment
    into your gravity.

GRAVITY

—

WROTE THIS SONG when I was nineteen. It's still one of the most requested songs I have and I will probably be playing it for as long as I live. The best part is that it doesn't even make me want to scratch my own eyes out.

Gravity was an expression of my first real encounter with heartbreak. The kind that you feel in your bones, that takes your breath away, and keeps you from sleeping. The kind that makes you lose your appetite and drive past his house at all hours of the night. It makes your grades drop, fills entire journals, and wears out cassette tapes of sad songs and drives your parents crazy 'cause you're being so mopey and pathetic. They can see you're just a dumdum eighteen-year-old who will get over this eventually, but you just can't possibly fathom *that* because you're so busy starring in your own Greek tragedy. Sadly, it's the exact same kind of heartbreak that can come back years later with the same characteristics and yet somehow even more venom.

I was maybe sixteen when I met LR, and he was everything I had always sort of fantasized about, but never in a million years thought I would experience firsthand. He was central casting for the darling romantic lead in any good teen romance flick: drop-dead gorgeous, popular, funny, brooding, not to mention our local sports hero. I, on the other hand, was perhaps less likely to be cast in that movie, fresh off my rejection letter from the auditions for the Mickey Mouse Club, picking up petting-zoo goat poop in my *Phantom of the Opera* sweatshirt for fun. It seemed unlikely that we would end up together, but life is funny that way.

I can't remember too many details of our courtship (if there was one at all), but we had a lot of mutual friends during our sophomore year of high school. I went to all the football and basketball games because that's generally what my small town did on Friday nights, and he (of course) was on those teams. A few of my close friends were on the cheerleading squad, which led to us ending up at a lot of the same parties, and I found myself gravitating toward him wherever he was in the room. The craziest part was that he seemed to be doing the same. During the summer before our junior year of high school, we started hanging out, and then making out, and both of those

First day of high school, August 1995

things I knew I liked *very* much. I felt he was so far out of my league, I really couldn't understand why he was interested in me. But he was, and so I considered myself a very lucky girl. He promptly took his seat at the center of my universe and my soft young heart fell madly in love.

There was something particularly formative about this experience for me, and I think a large part of that had to do with reciprocity. Because I was an awkward adolescent, and teased incessantly for my weight, I got used to feeling embarrassed about what I looked like. I was uncomfortable in my own skin and felt invisible to boys, unless it was to be the butt of a joke. I still fantasized, though. Awkward and all, I was no stranger to the insane fixation on romance that arrives with adolescence. I had "fallen in love" dozens of times with classmates and magazine photos and David Bowie in *Labyrinth* and all of the New Kids on the Block. But this was the first time anybody normal really had liked me back. This was a beautiful boy that every girl I knew hoped to get close to . . . who liked *me*. I was not used to this kind of attention, and especially not from someone like LR, once I got past the fear that this was some elaborate prank that would end up in pig's blood and ridicule at a prom somewhere, I relaxed into feeling safe and very proud of this love. I leaned into our relationship and the pride that came with wearing someone's attention. It made me feel powerful and beautiful, two things I now know we can't effectively cultivate from a place outside ourselves, but never the less, I was hooked.

That feeling is like a drug.

It's intoxicating to feel wanted by something you want.

There were really good parts about the relationship. We made everybody else laugh and made each other laugh even more. I adored his family. They were kind and warm and artsy and goofy, and welcomed me with open arms. He smelled good. He was an excellent kisser. He wrote me sweet notes in class and exposed me to really amazing music and his oddball artistic brain. I saw the sides of him that he didn't share outwardly when he was being everybody's favorite clown. His young artist mind, exploring drawing, painting, and sculpture, was just budding and trying to gain a foothold in his life, and I could see how privileged I was to be invited into such an intimate space. Our days at school were spent finding each other between classes and during breaks, swapping gossip and laughing about nothing. We both played sports, and outside of our practices and games, we spent every other spare moment on the phone or in each other's room, giggling and kissing and just being kids in love. And let's be honest, there is something really magical about loving someone, especially in the beginning, when they hijack your whole being and rewrite the synapses of your brain until they are conducting all the traffic. It's like everything is seen through the prism of that person, and it somehow makes everything sing.

I felt so incredibly special, so chosen, and for the first year I was over the moon. So much so that I ignored the parts of the relationship that weren't so good. We'd fight. He was moody. I was controlling. He was antagonistic, and I was a nag. Neither one of us knew how to communicate, so the seeds of discontent were planted and began to grow stronger. We began to resent each other, and the friction became more evident, but there was no way in hell I was going to acknowledge anything that would threaten the stability of what I considered to be the best thing that had ever happened to me.

Still clinging to the certainty of our future together, wearing my relationship like a crown, I tethered all of my self-esteem to it. If he loved me, it meant I was worth loving. When things shifted and he started to feel more distant toward the end of our senior year, I didn't know how to process that. A more mature me might have looked at our lives and realized we were heading in two completely different directions: I was off to UCLA and he was staying in Eureka. I might have figured that it would be best to leave space for other things. But instead, I grew out my horns and dug in my heels and deteriorated into what I consider to be the worst version of myself. My fear of losing him manifested as jealousy, possessive panic, and a grip so tight I would have strangled anything that required even the smallest amount of air to breathe. I was suspicious of every girl and every guy, for that matter, fiercely guarding something I felt was mine alone that everyone was trying to take away from me. We both were responsible for the ending of the relationship, but truly, whatever was sweet and true about finding each other in the beginning was long gone. I just wouldn't let it go.

Then he kissed someone else while I was out of town on a family trip.

I wasn't aware of this for about a week. When I got back from the trip, a girl in my choir class pulled me aside at school and gave me a letter telling me LR had been seen holding hands with a girl from a neighboring high school at a party. Along with the news, she also gave me an amethyst necklace. I know. I also think the necklace was a weird move.

I was leveled.

The shock and embarrassment of being told this intimate news by a marginal friend was really uncomfortable but I kept a brave face, thanked her for the crushing information and formal necklace, while internally the fires of hell rose up and my blood boiled. I was furious. Not only over the act itself, but because neither my boyfriend nor any of my friends had the guts to tell me. That afternoon I sped to his house in my little red Hyundai Excel, completely out of control. What happened after he answered the door is a total blur, although I know I was shaking and screaming at the top of my lungs, pushing him around and desperately trying to say something to him to make him feel as small as I did at that moment. I felt forgotten and ignored and disrespected and embarrassed and just so very, very sad. My worst fears had ultimately come true. I wanted to run screaming, backward in time, and do something differently that would have saved us from this, but all I could do was stare him down in that tiny little bedroom like a wild animal.

He didn't have much to say. I said the most hurtful things I could think of. We both cried, and when I ran out of mean words I went home. Over the next couple of weeks, there was no comfort for me anywhere. The truth of the matter was that things had changed and I didn't want them to.

There is no quick fix for the bitter pill of acceptance.

We were only a few weeks away from graduating, and soon enough I would be moving to Los Angeles, but that didn't soften this experience one little bit. One day not long after it had happened, I ducked out of history class because I just couldn't stop crying. My teacher came out to check on me in the hall and gave me advice that, at the time, made no sense whatsoever. He smiled knowingly and peeled a grapefruit while I sipped for air between sobs, and choked out words telling him what had happened. He didn't appear quite as appalled as I was hoping he would, and I was infuriated by his stupid adultness and inability to understand just how ruined I was. Now I can see he's a fucking genius.

He gave me a hug, handed me a section of grapefruit, and said, "Let time pass."

And then he said, "Eat more fruit."

He was right on both counts, but I wouldn't get it for many more years.

I dragged myself through the end of the school year and then ended up getting back together with my boyfriend just after graduation. I remember standing on the front porch at my house in the redwoods, feeling helpless as he stood before me promising that I was the only thing he'd ever really loved. It was the only thing in the world that I wanted to hear, so I agreed. He said he was so sorry and wanted me back and it was like a Christmas-morning feeling, but wrapped in sad. It was something coming true that I had desperately hoped for, but not without some new sense of knowing that this was a shell of what it had been. I knew something was gone that I couldn't get back, but I was just too sad to imagine up my own strength to continue to walk away, and too young to know what that would actually mean.

We were only officially back together for a few months, but the emotional tangle went on long after that, plenty long enough for me to begin to believe that I wasn't good enough to deserve and keep someone's love. That every relationship would end like this. My faith in trusting a partner has since returned, but it took more time than I care to admit to get over this initial blow. At the time, I thought it was *him* I was disappointed in, but I see now I did a lot of that damage to myself.

We broke up again just after I left for college, and the tortured saga continued for waaaaaay too long. I would come home from UCLA on my breaks and we would pick up old routines and I'd want to believe that things would turn around: that our love was big enough to transcend the five hundred miles and light-years of maturation required to make that relationship work. But of course it wasn't and we didn't and my heart would rip open every single time. We're always making everything slightly more difficult than it needs to be, aren't we?

Oh, us.

That teenage love was a skeletal version of what love feels like to me today, but my visceral reactions to losing it were mature expressions of pain and loss. And I think that because of the depth and complexities of those feelings, I was compelled for the very first time to turn to my piano to truly process my emotions. Gravity was written on my dad's old upright piano, one summer when I was on break from school, around a year after the breakup. I remember late-night composing, trying not to wake my sleeping father, crying over the piano keys.

I could clearly see my own pattern of returning to something that was not serving me, and yet I kept choosing to repeat it over and over. I felt so powerless and so deeply disappointed in my own inability to take control. It was easier to blame him for my pain, because then I didn't have to be responsible for myself. I didn't want it to be my fault. I wanted it to be something otherworldly that was drawing me back to him, my stuckness to not be a reflection of my own weakness, but something unavoidable, almost scientific. Gravity was the first time I really remember feeling catharsis through writing. It gave a home to feeling helpless, and I saw that there is power in the act of articulating your inner world. Giving my emotions a name changed them. The chemical makeup of the problem seemed to shift once it was dissected and placed somewhere. It was not a shortcut to healing, but at least a step in the right direction. He was clearly the force that was keeping me down, but I was the one who had to let go.

Putting that song together served as an emotional outlet where I could store my experience. I spent hours poring over the structure of it, and lots of parts of that process stay with me. I liked the evenness and repetition of the sounds of those opening chords, and I liked the simplicity of the phrasing of the verse lyric. The melody of the chorus made me feel melancholy and suited the sentiment, and the final line of the bridge was a triumphant discovery. I liked the juxtaposition of an ascending melodic line while saying the words *keeping me down*, and I also liked where the note sat in my register. People seem to be impressed with me hitting that note still to this day, but I'll share a secret with you: it's not really that high in my range. (It looks harder than it actually is, because I throw my head back.)

I don't think the song saved me from my heartbreak, but it did move me in a new direction, and I saw for the first time that sharing the truth of my own pain and vulnerability could also create a vehicle for connection with others. I played this song in some of my first performances and it seemed kinetic in its effect on people. I started to see how many of my fans were connecting to this sentiment of feeling overpowered by someone or something. Over the years, people have shared incredible stories of heartbreak, yes, but also of addiction, loss, death, and moving away from stagnancy in their lives. Those stories are moving and healing for me too. I am grateful to be a part of that exchange. I continue to see that the more I am willing to share the deepest and darkest parts of myself, the closer I feel to my life's work. Maybe that's why I don't tire of being requested to sing Gravity. It gave a lot back to me.

I am grateful to the boy who broke my heart for the very first time. I allowed myself to truly love something other than myself, and that is a beautiful experience, albeit painful. This song gave purpose to all that pain for me and somehow made it feel complete. Surrender is a healing sentiment to return to, and in the end, I'm glad that my heart was launched into the air by a careless kid, because I was gifted the opportunity of learning how to heal it once it hit the ground.

/ Radio City Music Hall, October 9, 2013

LOVE SONG

CHAPTER
three

Love Song

Head under water
And They tell me to breathe easy for a while
The breathing gets harder
Even I know That
Made room for me, but it's too soon to see
If I'm happy in your hands
I'm unusually hard to hold onto.

Blank stares at blank pages
No easy way to say This
You mean well, but you make This hard on me
I'm ~~damn~~ NOT gonna write you a
        - LOVE SONG -

Cause you asked for it, cause you need one
you see
I'm not gonna write you a love song
Cause you tell me it's make or breaking This
If you're on your way
I'm not gonna write you to stay
If all you have is leaving
I'm gonna need a better reason
to write you a love song
        today.

LOVE SONG

—

THE STORY OF LOVE SONG has morphed over the years into an incredibly oversimplified version of the truth. I think I even helped perpetuate it. It would take too long to correct every person who assumes they know the story. But this succinct version of the "truth" must have been sent out to every interviewer I've ever spoken to, because they all say the same thing:

The big bad record company demanded that I write them a love song and I, being the cheeky, indignant young songstress that I am, thumbed my nose at them and gave them the anti–love song. Huzzah!

Their story isn't false; it's a half-truth. I gave up trying to assert the entirety of the story because it is, like most things in life, more nuanced and complicated than a distilled one-liner that reads, "She walked into iTunes with her dukes up" (a phrase I have actually read). Don't get me wrong—I *like* the idea of being some sort of modern musical Lone Ranger, but that's not really how it happened. Love Song served as a beacon to help me find my way back to my own artistry at a time when I had lost sight of what that meant. And it was the culmination of years of experience.

In 2003, I was newly graduated from UCLA and still living in Los Angeles, working as a waitress and playing lots of gigs on the side. I had a degree in communications, which might *sound* like something, but no actual things require this degree. It's like studying the history of Jennifer Aniston's hairstyle—a lot of fun, but not that practical. I had no idea what I was going to do with the rest of my life. At twenty-three years old, when I sat with the daunting task of trying to choose some sort of path forward, I got overwhelmed. So I just focused on having fun. I knew that I loved playing music, and I took a job in a bar with a great beer selection and flexible scheduling so I could devote myself to playing my gigs and avoiding my future. While I figured it out, I might as well drink a lot of expensive beer and nurture friendships with people who were just as deliciously aimless as I was.

I used the money I made to pay for rehearsal spaces, a rotating cast of band members, shitty keyboards, and, judging from photos of myself at that time, a variety of head scarves. At

Playing a show at Hotel Café

the time, I probably had about seven or eight completed songs and many seeds of song ideas that were stylistically all over the map. As cringeworthy as it can be, I still sort of love this stage in a young artist's development. There's something sweet and untamed about trying to develop a craft you don't totally understand yet. It is the musical equivalent of playing dress-up, trying things on hoping eventually you get to the bottom of the trunk and find something that fits and feels good. Sometimes you stumble into some happy accidents that stick. If you're me, you also stumble into writing a pop-reggae tune about making out. I'll go ahead and leave that in the vault for another time. I tried every-

thing. Country songs. Girly punk rock. Moody down-tempos.
Folky poetry songs. Jazz. Musical theater. I tried to write hybrids
of all of the above. I used the word *moonbeam* a lot. It was certainly not a very subtle or refined time in my writing, but it was
playful and pure and it brought me closer to finding myself. As I
mimicked other people's music, I uncovered facets of myself as
a writer, and eventually collected a handful of songs that I had
written on my own and was willing to share as I got acquainted
with the singer-songwriter circuit in LA.

Starting out, I played anywhere and everywhere. I opened
for magicians at loungey beachside bars, and played on back
porches of coffee shops that served warm beer in a can. I played
fancy backyards for private parties, and crunchy weekend
women's festivals. I played stages that had stripper poles but no
strippers (sad face), and kosher Chinese restaurants that served
egg rolls to their patrons while I tried to think of between-song
banter for people eating egg rolls. So many shows. I put together
a small band that was in flux for the first year and a half or so,
and we would play a few of my original songs and a handful of
covers because I hadn't yet written enough music to quite fill
an entire set. If you had come to a very early show of mine, you
might have been lucky enough to catch me wearing a skull-
cap and a hemp necklace, playing I Will Survive to the pre-
programmed drumbeat on my keyboard while my buddy the
djembe player beatboxed to help the "groove." Well-intended,
but maybe not one of my most musical moments. However,
playing shows made me hungry to write even more music, and
so I started doing more of that, growing my repertoire of songs.

Between 2003 and 2005, I met some musicians I truly connected with, and the show and my band began to take shape, to exhibit consistency and more musicality. After my previous encounters (with, for example, the bass player who came to shows super stoned and played facing the wall instead of the audience), finding these people was like finding an oasis in a desert. That first year of shows was a crash course in putting together a band and building my business, and I had no idea what I was doing. I made plenty of mistakes, but eventually found my way toward good, kind, funny, talented human beings who are still some of my best friends in the world.

Looking back on those early days now, I realize I had no perspective on where my music was headed, but as time passed, the picture revealed itself slowly, slowly, slowly. I went from playing in front of twelve people who were doing me a personal favor by coming to the show, to playing for hundreds of people who had come for the music (and, potentially, the head scarves). I was amazed to see that I was actually building something within the Los Angeles music scene. The crowds and the venues were getting bigger and better, and it became clear that there was a demand from my small but dedicated fan base to have recordings of my music.

I recorded and released my first album independently in January 2004. It was called *Careful Confessions*, and I recorded it with a good friend and artist, Gabriel Mann, who had produced the records *Pitch-Slapped* and *Dysfunktional Family Album* for my college a cappella group, Awaken. (A cappella groups love puns.) Gabe has the curliest hair in the world, a dry wit, great talent, and works fast. He's a studio nine-to-fiver, my favorite kind of producer. There are a lot of musicians and producers out there who love "hanging" in the studio, and I promise they're all cooler than me. I'm too high-strung and too cheap to enjoy lounging on a couch that costs $1,500 a day. I like to "hang" at home, or at a cozy bar, or with tiny ponies on a farm. When I'm in the studio, I want to work. Gabe and I were very compatible that way. *Careful Confessions* consisted of seven studio recordings and a handful of lo-fi live recordings, the best of what I had written up until that point. It took maybe a month to record and mix everything, and I began to get acquainted with a process that would become a large part of my life as an artist.

When things are going well at the studio, life is euphoric. It's like being on the world's greatest drug. I remember hearing my own voice recorded professionally, singing my own songs for the first time in that little studio under the freeway in Culver City. It sent electricity through my body and filled me with a soaring sense of possibility. I loved the sound of it in those huge studio headphones that make everything sound wide and rich and thick. I would turn the volume way up and close my eyes and disappear into the sonic landscape that was being built around my voice. It was magical.

There are also the crippling minutiae and meticulous detail of recording that account for my love-hate relationship with the process. There are infinite choices to make about how to capture and present a song, and there's no right answer. For example, my song Come Round Soon has had many incarnations, each with a very distinct flavor. It began as a lo-fi demo with a hip-hop feel, then became a swingy, up-tempo pop song with loads of background vocals and cello. After that, it became a driving, Police-inspired rock tune with tons of electric guitar and a straight-ahead feel. These days, I play it solo on distorted electric guitar, pretending I'm Patti Smith. The same song becomes entirely new just by changing the instrumentation and feel. There is great freedom in producing a song, but at that age, I found those possibilities exhausting instead of exciting. I was paralyzed, lacking both the vocabulary and the knowledge of what I wanted.

I have a vivid memory of recording Gravity, a song I always had played solo on piano, and having the band come in to play. We were piled in Gabe's little studio, Josh Day on drums and Travis Carlton on bass, playing the song through for the first time. The most straightforward approach, with the backbeat on the two and the four, felt generic to me, but that was all I could decipher. I had no idea how to steer the ship in another direction, because I didn't know any other directions. I sat on the arm of the couch while the band and Gabe waited for me to have an opinion. I started to panic. Not only was the overall direction of the song still muddy in my mind, I literally didn't know what words to use to tell the musicians what I wanted. I don't read music, and I don't know music theory. All I could say at the time were opaque things like, "I want this part to feel dreamy," or, "This should really change shape." Helpful, right? I felt stupid and inarticulate next to all these talented people who spoke the language of music in a way I couldn't.

Everyone was extremely patient with me and did their best to intuit where I was yearning for the song to go. They eventually found their way toward the rolling, atmospheric arrangement of that song. The first time Josh tried the new groove, with brushes on the snare drum emphasizing the offbeat, I felt a wave of relief. It wasn't my idea, but I knew when I heard it, it was exactly what I wanted.

I have learned over the years that the "not knowing" is part of the beauty of making music, and that vocabulary is important, but not crucial in communication. Only patience is crucial in communication. Recording is exploration. You take a piece of music and excavate, searching for the shape the song wants to take in that moment. You use wonderful musicians, producers, and engineers who help you navigate those waters and hopefully also help you remember that it doesn't have to feel precious or scary. You try things that don't work as you hunt for what does. And sometimes you even find it.

Now I had an album. In a hard plastic JEWEL CASE! It made me feel official. I sold *Careful Confessions* at my shows and on my brand-new website (!!!), and also registered it with CDBaby.com, an online music store for independent artists. By the time it came out, I had already played at least a hundred shows, and had completed one two-week tour of East Coast colleges opening for Maroon 5, friends of mine from college. I could sense that something was beginning to happen around me. Through my site and CDBaby.com I was eventually getting album orders from across the country—then all over the world. I couldn't believe it. I spent countless hours at my little kitchen table handling the details of booking shows, e-mailing fans, returning MySpace messages, signing my albums, and labeling the packages to be sent out. I had to reorder the CD from the printer. I sold maybe a few thousand of those records with my own two hands. I started to consider the notion that I could maybe make a living doing this. It seemed strange and self-indulgent to even entertain that fantasy, but I was witnessing things unfold organically that made it almost seem possible. I had been so busy avoiding my own future I almost overlooked the fact that it was staring right back at me. I quit my waitressing job and started calling myself a musician. It was a proud day.

None of this would have been possible without my roommate and best friend, Chad Joseph. Chad and I met in 2001, bonding over a conversation during which we commiserated over the fact that none of our friends at UCLA had noticed we had both been gone for the *entire* previous year studying abroad. (An excited "How was your summer?!" conversation inevitably transformed into a sheepish "Sorry I didn't realize you weren't here last year" conversation.) Chad is one of the funniest people I've ever known, a sweetheart from the Valley with perfect teeth and a huge heart. We lived together in a little two-bedroom apartment in Santa Monica when all of this was happening around me, and Chad took on the role of unofficial manager during that time. I don't know how I would have moved forward without him. Chad did a little bit of everything. Before *Careful Confessions* was first printed, he would stay up all night burning CDs on his laptop and handwriting the labels so I could sleep. He organized the mailing list, answered a

bazillion e-mails, helped me load up the car with my equip-
ment. At the shows, he sold CDs and handled inquiries about
bookings and whatever else came up. This is the tip of the ice-
berg of the kinds of things Chad did for me at that time, and he
did all of it for no pay. We both thought we were headed toward
a professional relationship as manager and artist.

After eight months of working independently on *Careful Confessions*, in August 2004, my record landed on the
desk of Jordan Feldstein. He was a young, hungry manager
from Los Angeles, and after my first tour with his then baby
band and my college buddies, Maroon 5, he had listened to
the record and was interested in representing me. Jordan was
connected, fearless, and driven, putting touring opportunities
and a big-picture plan in front of me. He was not, however,
interested in a co-management configuration. Chad and I had
an awkward meeting with him and a long painful heart-to-
heart in private. We decided that I needed to try and work
with someone who had more experience. Chad was selfless
through that entire transition. I struggled terribly with feeling
disloyal, but Chad's grace and generosity made me feel like
he understood. I realize it was ultimately the right decision,
and I'm happy to say that Chad was then by my side for years
as my tour manager, and was a crucial part of my early years
as an artist.

Jordan's tenacity would prove to be incredibly important, especially in the early stages of my career. Those days
were fraught with a sort of "against the odds" kind of spirit.
Although I was having some success with my audience, I didn't

fit in any particular mold, and that was challenging for out-siders in the industry to understand. Hell, it was challenging for *me* to understand. I played pop music, but I didn't reflect the existing aesthetic of any of the successful female artists of the time. I wasn't Britney Spears or Jessica Simpson. I wasn't Tori Amos or Norah Jones. Nobody knew what to do with me. Journalists and reviewers were confused. Industry profession-als were wary of taking a chance on me. I found it infuriating: I didn't want to be like anyone else. I wore T-shirts and jeans, drank and swore on stage, and wrote songs about Cinderella getting drunk. To be fair, I'm not surprised that my onstage per-sona was mildly confusing, but I resented being made to feel *wrong* because of it.

I thank God I had Jordan in my corner fighting for me. He never once suggested I do anything to change my aesthetic, musical or otherwise. He treated a lot of the "constructive" criticism as nonsense and encouraged me to continue to be myself. With his guidance we charged forward toward our first major goal—gaining the attention of a record label in hopes of taking my music to the next level.

This "looking for a record label" thing looks different for everyone and there are no rules. I can only speak to my own experience, which consisted of a handful of "showcases," where record company folks (or lawyers or agents) were invited to a series of private performances in various rehearsal spaces to see me play four or five songs live with my band. There is nothing natural about knowing you're being judged and evalu-ated for investment, and I was not especially cool under pres-

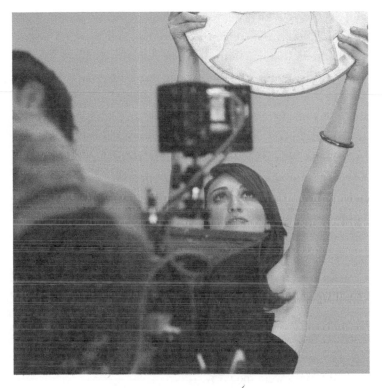

/ *Love Song music-video shoot*

sure. I remember one of these first showcases was set up for a
young lawyer, and I pulled out all the stops. I rented a small
rehearsal room in West LA and decorated it with twinkle lights,
folding chairs, and a makeshift bar with bottles of beer on ice.
I dressed up, made jokes, and had the most awkward twenty
minutes of my life. I was so uncomfortable, fumbling through

chitchat and not knowing where to look in the room while I was singing. I barely remember the performance. I think it's impossible to wear that much desperation and still act like a human. When the first person passed on working with me, it stung, but I tried to chalk it up to just not being a good fit for each other. But the rejections kept coming until no became the answer I came to expect.

These showcases were the first taste of really seeing myself as a product to be "sold," and that bitter pill did not go down easy. Especially since no one was buying. It's hard not to believe people when they're just so incredibly *specific* about what they don't like about you.

I was told many things I started to believe:

My songs weren't good.

I was "just a voice."

My tube tops didn't fit.

My personality onstage was distracting.

My band wasn't good.

My songs were too jazzy.

My style was bad.

My sound wasn't cool.

On and on.

My self-doubt was raging, but I continued to play shows and do my level best to shake it off and keep focused on all of those devout early fans who kept me going. They were so generous. They spent their time, love, and money on my shows, and made me feel like somebody wanted what I had to give. Somehow they saw past my tube tops and terrible songs and wanted to be in the room. They made me want to be in the room too. They guided me through the gauntlet of those first steps into the industry and steered me toward steady footing and something that felt whole and sane.

Thank you forever, sweet ninjas.

One night toward the end of 2004, Pete Giberga, an A&R representative from Epic Records, was invited by my manager to a show of mine at the Temple Bar in Santa Monica, a moody, bohemian little club near the beach that I had played at dozens of times. I had no idea ho wao in the room and I suppose my performance was liberated because of it. As far as I was concerned, the only people in the room were my friends and fans, and so I was afforded the luxury of being observed while I truly enjoyed myself. I was introduced to Pete after the show, and I was shocked to hear that he had *enjoyed* it. He wanted to have a follow-up meeting. I agreed, and internally steeled myself to hear that my sound needed work or I needed to write better songs or change my name or shave my head or lose weight or whatever else was wrong with me.

I was woozy walking into the enormous Sony Building in Santa Monica for my meeting. This is was what Jordan and I had been working toward and what I had wanted for so long, but I was skeptical. Putting myself out there to be criticized so many times made me nervous about exposing myself to what had already proven to be extremely painful. The meeting went really well, and spending time with Pete over the next couple of months made the idea of taking the next step seem palatable. I liked his straight talk and the fact that he wore hoodies and sneakers. Pete loves music, and believes in people. He's also a rare breed of industry professional who still believes in the virtue of spending time and energy *developing* an artist. He made very clear that this was going to be a long process and that there were no guarantees. I decided to believe him. To this day he is a dear and trusted friend who only wears dress shoes at funerals and weddings.

I was flown to New York with Jordan to meet with the president of the label at the time, Steve Barnett, and talk about the prospect of being an Epic artist. I felt incredibly young and inexperienced on that trip. I sat next to Jordan at LAX waiting to board the plane and confessed to him that I didn't know what to say in the meeting. He said, "Say whatever you want to say." I wished I knew what that might be. His office was in the corner on what felt like the six hundredth floor, and I walked down the halls of Epic Records taking in the plaques on the wall. This was Michael Jackson's label. Fiona Apple's. Pearl Jam's. Rage Against the Machine's. George Michael's. My palms were sweating.

Steve was kind and forthright in our meeting, and I appreciated that. We talked about the music I had already written and the kind of artist I hoped to become. His interest in me seemed polite and measured, but he was gracious. I got the sense that it was a reluctant handshake in front of me, but he did leave me feeling that there was an opportunity to move forward here if I wanted to take it, as long as I was willing to try cowriting with professional songwriters. It stung more than a little bit to hear that my own body of work wasn't enough for him to sign off on me, but I told him that I would try. No promises though, as I had had several poor attempts at writing with others under my belt already. My anxiety about sharing my newborn ideas was very strong, and my fear of getting bowled over and taken in directions I didn't want to go was even stronger. During the meeting, I racked my brain for intelligent questions to ask, but ultimately stayed pretty quiet, too overwhelmed to say a whole lot, as I agreed to the parameters and the negotiations progressed. I could sense the rumblings of a seismic shift in my life. It made me really nervous.

Several months later I signed my record deal in my lawyer's office in Santa Monica. As much as I had wanted it and worked for it, it felt like things were moving so fast. My overactive imagination was playing out only worst-case scenarios. I would get pressured into being something I wasn't. I would become famous and hate it. I would be bullied and disempowered and stuck there forever. A lot of those horrible things oddly enough *would* eventually happen, but my mistake that day was in underestimating my own ability to handle it. I wish I could go back, give myself a hug, and tell myself that even when bad things happened, I was going to be okay. That was April 15, 2005, and I spent the rest of that year forging ahead, hoping for the best, and going to writing sessions with professional songwriting teams.

I have since realized that I would rather eat steak knives and a bag of hair.

This is another process that has no rules; still, my cowriting sessions generally all resembled one another. I would go to the home studio or writing room of a rich and relatively pleas-ant person with expensive, alkaline-infused bottled water and beige furniture, who had plaques on the wall commemorating gold and platinum records that they had written for gold and platinum selling artists like Kelly Clarkson or Avril Lavigne. We would exchange pleasantries for a little while and then some-body would go and drag music into the room. My armpits would start sweating as a guitar would get picked up and a few chords would get strummed or a half-finished prerecorded track that "sounded like me" would get played, and I would be asked to share my thoughts or build on it somehow. I was like a deer in headlights. My stomach would tighten and my cheeks would flush as the people pleaser in me felt immense pressure to val-idate the idea but the artist in me wanted to run screaming. The truth is, I didn't want to write music that way. The process didn't make me feel connected or inspired, but I was too wor-ried about disappointing this big machine that was now moving forward on my behalf to say anything. I was waiting for some-one else to give me permission to make my own decisions, and that was my greatest mistake.

Just for the record, I want to be clear that this is not a judgment on the talent or integrity of these types of writers, or even the particular writers I met. Incredible songs have come out of cowriting for all kinds of artists, but in my opinion the most connected material comes out of organic human connec-tion, and you just don't know when or where that will sprout up. I had a long series of unsuccessful meetings and half songs and very awkward afternoons, but the final straw came in Santa Monica at a little cottage near the beach. I had a session with a very successful writer who shall remain nameless in this book. Let's just call him Dick Douche. He sauntered into the room and indulged me with about six minutes of vapid chitchat and feigned interest in my life, then slid a typed-up list of song titles that I could choose from over to me on the coffee table. It was full of names like 2 Good 4 U and Better 2 B Without U, and no, he wasn't Prince. I was panicked at the idea of getting through a session that had started this badly, but before I had even read to the bottom of the list, he had decided that since I was young I should write something about "fun," so he excitedly suggested Just Have Fun! and before I knew it, he had delighted himself and skipped out of the room to go record his idea.

It didn't even matter that I was in the room. He hadn't taken the time to listen to a single song I had written. He wasn't concerned with who I was as a writer or what my goals were in moving forward. He made me feel invisible. All of those sessions had made me feel that way. I sat stunned on the couch, choking back tears and making small talk with his writing partner while I waited for the session to end. I think his partner had started to clue in on my extreme discomfort, and he eventually gingerly walked me out to my car and gave me a hug. I don't remember the other guy coming back in to say goodbye. I drove away in tears, exhausted, embarrassed, and feeling two inches tall. It occurred to me how precious and private the act of writing music was to me. It was excruciating sharing that part of myself.

/ Little Voice *album photo shoot, 2007*

I felt like I was being asked to invite complete strangers into my sacred, secret fort and that none of them were respecting what I had already built. It might have been unrefined, rough around the edges, close to collapsing . . . but I had spent all the years of my life constructing it. Reggae and all. It was innocent and childlike. It was mine. If I was going to share it with someone, I needed to feel like they could at least acknowledge it and, more importantly, help me protect it. I was absolutely a rookie songwriter and had maybe thirty songs to my name, a lot of them terrible, but I was developing my own voice as a writer. My songs were my blood cells as far as I was concerned, and the idea of allowing someone to toy with them sent me into toxic shock. It didn't help that I was being paired with people who spent all day every day in writing sessions and had naturally developed more of a business-minded relationship with the writing process itself. For me, music was still too precious. Too raw. Too private. I can see now how I contributed to those sessions being unsuccessful. The truth is that I wasn't yet comfortable enough in my own skin to be open to the *possibility* of creating something with anyone. Collaboration requires trust, and first and foremost you have to trust yourself. I just wasn't there yet.

The last stop on that train of potential collaboration was Eric Rosse, whose quiet and patient nature left space for me to be in the room. He is a talented and accomplished writer and producer and had produced two of my favorite Tori Amos records of all time. I think that gave me an inroad into believing he could be a safe place. The first thing we did was sit and talk for a while. He was genuinely interested in my story. He asked questions about me, about my music. I felt a tiny part of me open up and start to let something in, and though we met as potential cowriters, Eric ended up producing the entire record. He was encouraging of my songwriting ideas, and I felt validated and inspired to dig deeper and finish them on my own. He gave good suggestions and was an attentive listener— more so than any of the other writers I had met with. He and I ended up developing the kind of dynamic relationship that proves both parties care very much about what they're making. This means we fought hard. I cried a lot. (I think he did too, but didn't let me see.) It certainly wasn't easy, but Eric pushed me in ways I needed to be pushed and I am grateful for all of it.

All that frustration leading up to this point with the writers, the label, and the process itself was a catalyst for me in digging back into my own storytelling. I wrote Love Song not long after that last writing debacle with Mr. Douche, at a rehearsal space in Los Angeles. I shared a small storage unit with some of my best friends in a band called Raining Jane, and I was using it as a writing room in the mornings. Our space was basically a teeny-tiny little roll-down-garage-door metal box, filled to the brim with a random smattering of instruments, twinkle lights, road cases, merchandise boxes, plastic tubs, half-drunk bottles of liquor, and bungee cords. We split the cost of the room for close to two years, and both bands would practice there and store whatever bullshit wouldn't fit in the trunk of our cars. It worked out well until Public Storage found out we were playing music there and they eventually shut us down. The end of an era.

It was sunny and I drove to the rehearsal space in the morning with a coffee from 7-Eleven and walked down the corridor to the dingy but cozy little room that felt like the inside of a garbage can. I was numb. It had been months of bad meetings and confusion and insecurity and doubting my own abilities and trying to remember the way it feels to write something you love. There's an innocence that comes with writing songs for no reason, and I was so very far from that point of connection. I sat down at my keyboard and literally prayed to God to help me write something that brought me back to a place I could feel.

Who I am as a songwriter had always been the most pure part of myself. She connects me to my deepest truth and says things I don't always feel the courage to say in my own life. I felt so much distance from her in that moment, I just wanted help to find her again. I asked for guidance in writing something that wasn't for anyone but me and my muse. I asked for the strength to release feeling responsible for making anyone else happy with what I created. I placed my hands on the keys and the opening chord progression came spilling out from somewhere. The majority of that song was written in about thirty minutes, which is *incredibly* fast for me. Most of my songs take hours and hours, if not weeks and months and sometimes even years. It was a gift that I desperately needed that day and I still don't think I had much to do with writing it. That's just plain ol' magic and God.

In my next session with Eric, I shared the idea. It felt connected for me, but that meant nothing about whether or not it would connect with anyone else. I had shared so many ideas at this point that hadn't landed; this could easily have been more of the same. He told me it was really good and smiled, suggesting I repeat the hook in the chorus a second time. I played with structure and finished the song in the next day or so. I felt myself exhale for the first time in a long time.

I had poured my frustration into those lyrics, giving voice to how small I felt. That song was a culmination of years of being criticized and misunderstood. Months of unfulfilling writing sessions that left me feeling vulnerable, inadequate, and worst of all, invisible. This song was what came out of my struggle to find my own voice again. The lyrics were so literal I thought that the label was going to be upset with me, and that no one would be able to relate to the story because it was so specifically mine. I was certain that it would get lumped into the bevy of discarded songs, but I didn't care. I felt creatively energized. Eric and I made a demo and nothing could have prepared me for the phone calls I got after we sent it off. My label and my manager were elated. They were jumping up and down over that song. I was shocked. I had to break the news to Pete that the song was about them. He laughed and laughed.

I'm not saying that Love Song is a perfect piece of writing, but it saved *me* in a lot of ways. At a crucial moment in my life, it allowed me a glimpse of that sacred connection that happens only every once in a while with songwriting, and reminded me it hadn't been extinguished. I think in some ways it prepared me for stepping into the professional realm on a larger scale. There is an enormous amount of toxic nonsense to wade through as an artist, and if you lose sight of what is at the center of it all, you run the risk of losing yourself completely. Love Song became a barometer of truth for me and reminded me of who I was as a writer and an artist at a time when I really needed to know. If nothing else, that moment of clarity would help me be more patient in waiting for the next one.

And that's the bigger story of Love Song.

I don't share all of that with everyone. It's not only that it's a lot of information; much of it is just so personal. It doesn't need to be written about in a magazine or spoken of on the radio in a five-minute interview. I can share it in the pages of this book because it feels safe here, like I'm among friends. In a way, the entirety of these pages is an extension of that childhood fort I'm still trying to protect. And now you're in on the secret. So . . . if you happen to catch the next time someone gets that cheeky look on their face and says to me, "So is it true that you wrote Love Song for your record label when they told you to write them a love song?"

You will mostly likely see me smile and answer yes.

But you'll know better.

BEAUTIFUL GIRL

CHAPTER
four

2:41:30:06   A006_C037

Beautiful Girl

You want to walk into the room
like that other girl does
The one that's always making everybody
  fall in love
You see, girl you're a lot like me.
She rearranges all the light in the room
  So you're always in the shadows
Well, that's what it feels like to you
  Baby, I've been there too.
I know how much it can sometimes hurt
  you feel like the whole world has made you
      the ugly girl.
But take it from me that you have to
      see it first.
So, before you trade in your summer skin
  for those high-heeled shoes
  to make 'em wanna be with you
Let me remind you one more time that just
  maybe you're beautiful but you just can't see
      So why don't you trust me?
  And they'll see it too,
          you BEAUTIFUL girl, you.

Dear Sara,

I know when your friend Matt dropped a quarter in the schoolyard and you put your foot on it to tease him, acting like you weren't going to let him get it, you were trying to be funny. You didn't know what to say when he yelled, "I'd need a bulldozer to move *that* leg." You laughed because you were uncomfortable, but your stomach turned and you cried when you got into the bathroom. You look in the mirror and you don't really like what you see.

At the school dance in seventh grade, you will be brave enough to ask the other Matt to dance. He'll run away from you screaming, making you feel very awkward and lonely. When you ask his friend Kenny why he did that, he'll say, "Matt thinks you're fat, ugly, and a snob." You'll write that down in your journal, which you are beginning to do more of these days. You spend a lot of time and mental energy comparing yourself to the other kids in your class. You think every other girl is cuter than you, and you *have* noticed that you are bigger than most of them. You're ashamed of that. You wish you could just disappear sometimes. I'm very glad that you don't.

You are beautiful.

You have a kind heart and your sensitivity is swiftly growing in ways you will never understand right now, and someday you will be so glad for all of this. Being a kid is hard sometimes,

St. Bernard's Elementary class picture, fourth grade, 1989

because kids are just miniature people and being a person is really hard. That part doesn't change, unfortunately. But right now you are particularly innocent and vulnerable, and I'm sorry that you feel punished and excluded sometimes.

You are learning empathy, and what it feels like to be left out. This is going to make you want to be the kind of person who makes room for people who feel like outsiders, and it's going to serve you well. It's going to guide you toward people who love you for who you are, so hang in there. Trust me that things are moving in the right direction.

Love,
Sara

Dear Sara,

You have fallen in deep and desperate love with about six different boys this week. It will happen again next week. You are at a new high school with new friends, and the circle of people you hang out with is shifting constantly. *My So-Called Life* is the best thing that has ever happened to you. You believe that you practically *are* Angela and you dyed your hair in the bathroom at your mom's new house to feel closer to Claire Danes, or you, or whatever. You are mortified by the "white spots" on your two front teeth that are calcium deposits that will bother you for the rest of your life. You will figure out that they are especially prominent if you acciden- tally sleep with your mouth open and so you will scotch-tape your mouth shut at night for a while. You are getting used to the fact that since the divorce you have two homes now. You don't like dealing with the back-and-forth, but you also don't know how to talk about that, and so you just don't.

You started drinking this year. You were one of the last of your friends to try it, because you wanted to be a responsible person. Then you were shocked and kind of disappointed when it was actually really fun. You had your first drink, red wine in a plastic cup, on the beach at night in the pitch-black dark and your stomach felt warm, your muscles relaxed, and silliness seeped up from your blood and then you had to pee. You ran far enough down the beach so no one could see you, and then took your shoes, pants, and underwear all the way off and left them in a folded pile while you laughed out loud, ran a few steps farther down the beach, and peed. It made no sense, but it will be a story you tell forever about the first time you got drunk.

You stay at your best friend Kona's a lot during the weekends because her mom works nights and is gone most of the time. You get buzzed on jugs of Carlo Rossi Burgundy wine with Kona and your new friends and you will all call yourselves the Carlo Rossi Posse. You are a quiet observer a lot because you feel intimidated by how much you admire them. They are artists and philosophers and writers and musicians and they are a precursor to you finding their likenesses again and again in your life, but you don't see that yet.

You've convinced yourself that your true love must be right around the corner. It's not. Or at least the corner is a hell of a lot bigger than you think it is. You keep finding yourself infatuated with someone new who doesn't feel the way you do, and then somebody finally does feel the way you do next year. Every rejection you encounter will be twisted into a story you tell yourself that ends with "I am ugly," and the relationship you end up having will do the same thing. You feel overlooked and plain and embarrassed and you break your own heart over and over again by placing so much value on this particular kind of love. You feel incessantly unseen.

I see you.

You are beautiful.

You are innocent and naïve and you are exploring your adolescence. You believe in the good in people and you believe just about anything is possible. That feeling gets harder to hold on to as we age, so I am especially fond of that in you now. You have surrounded yourself with people who make you feel inspired by art, music, movies, and laughter, and you are ingesting it and storing that sense of awe and excitement for a little later down the road. You crave sharing love because you have a lot of love to share, and your teenage brain can only see a certain distance because that's how it's wired. There is so much incredible road ahead and so much love waiting for you, you can't even imagine how gorgeous it all is. I'm glad that you had experiences where you felt unseen, because those delicate moments are fine-tuning your natural instinct to be introspective. Your observer self is growing and will be a dear friend to you as you begin to tell your stories with music, and it will allow you to see things and articulate your experience in a way that makes other invisible people feel seen. Drinking makes you feel a whole bunch of things that I wish you felt sober, and you will eventually. You are exactly where you belong, and your tender heart is precious.

Love,
Sara

Dear Sara,

You are living in an apartment off campus at UCLA with a bunch of girls. It is your first year out of the dorms and the apartment has tall ceilings and rounded Spanish doorways and bougainvillea growing over the car park. You float on the excitement surrounding your new independent life, away from your parents and anyone who's known who you've already been. You feel like anything and everything is possible and it makes your heart race in both good and bad ways. You are reinventing yourself, and right now you are using the girls around you as a background to build your own self image. Most of them are very petite blonde girls, and you are having a hard time with how you don't really fit that mold. Many of them are joining sororities and you went to that one event and tried hard to impress all of the girls in the house and did. They asked you back to join the sorority, but you politely declined because you didn't really feel like yourself. You are searching for a way to connect to who you are in your soul, and you aren't finding it easily.

You spend a lot of time hating yourself and your body and you have started drinking a lot on weekends and throwing up the food you eat after drinking. You get positive reinforcement for that period of time where you restricted your eating so much and ran around the track obsessively, so you are getting the wrong message. You lose a little bit of weight and everyone says how good you look, and that feels nice and stresses you out even more. You don't get attention from boys hardly at all. You have started using sexuality as currency to attract their attention, and that doesn't feel very good, but you're very drunk when you do it, so it's hard to tell which part is the part that doesn't feel so good. The next few years are going to be really hard on your self-esteem.

You will move to Italy next year to study abroad and break your dangerous habit of being obsessive and disciplined about food by going in the opposite direction and eating anything and everything. You'll gain close to twenty pounds while you are there and shock yourself with how you look in pictures. You won't really recognize yourself, but that will make sense, because the entirety of your experience in Italy feels surreal and strange. Feeling fat becomes one of the lesser of the uncomfortable things you will experience. You will discover that music is the only thing in the world that makes your soul feel understood. You make some conclusions about yourself that define the next chapter of your life: You are a songwriter. You are fat. You are ugly.

Only one of those is true.

You are beautiful.

You are trying your best to make sense of a whole new world and a whole new self. It's scary to take steps toward independence, and I wish I could help you feel softer toward yourself while you explore what that actually means. The dynamic nature of your experience right now is completely normal, and those high highs and low lows are a ride that you will get used to and learn to appreciate. I know you are overwhelmed by your own emotions a lot these days, and it makes you angry with yourself. But a bird's-eye view shows that there is a bottleneck building up, shepherding you toward your own discovery of songwriting as a part of your essence, not just a hobby. And you aren't alone. You are about to find a maze of people who share a love of the thing that will be your life-boat: music. They will be a bunch of silly, big-hearted, lifelong friends who are waiting around the corner. You are about to dance ridiculous choreography while you sing a cappella songs that make you think your heart might burst open from happiness. Soon, you will start really writing your own music, and you will see such depth in yourself that you didn't know was there. It will fill you up. You will tell your story of feeling invisible to love, and it will comfort other people who feel the same way, and it will make you feel connected to something bigger than yourself. You are on the right path, and you are exactly where you need to be.

Love,
Sara

Dear Sara,

It's April 15, 2005. Today you walked into your new lawyer's office in Santa Monica and signed a record deal, then
you walked the fourteen blocks home to your tiny upstairs
apartment and cried. You feel miserable and guilty about
the fact that you aren't celebrating this milestone moment,
but you feel like you have just given something away that you
won't be able to get back. In your mind you have just jumped
without a net. You call your mom and realize for the first time
that she can't make it better.

You have spent the last year of your life in and out of deep
anxiety and depression, and you are seriously afraid that you
might be crazy. This will continue for some time. Sometimes
you have disassociation with your body and your thoughts
get so loud that you feel like you can't see straight and can't
engage with the room around you. It frightens you and makes
you feel very alone. You don't tell very many people about this.

You try therapy for the first time. It was impossibly hard
to start down that path, because surrendering to how bad
things got in your brain is embarrassing for you and makes
you feel weak. The lady you end up finding is a frumpy, cold,
older woman with glasses who smells like very strong air
freshener. You secretly hate her. She says hardly anything
at all, and it makes you very uncomfortable and so you just
start talking out loud to fill up the silence. She is not a very

good therapist, but filling up the space between the two of you with your thoughts teaches you to articulate them. The emotions that felt overwhelming before become puzzles to try and solve. You start to slowly climb out of the darkness, and the relief you feel is as wide as the whole galaxy.

You have a blurry image of what you want out of your career, and you are in the middle of building the foundation. Playing shows around Los Angeles, you are also making your first record. You seek approval and validation from just about everyone around you and lose your own opinion along the way.

You stumble into moments that trigger a triumphant feeling but end up making you feel tricked. In a studio in New York City you will be told, "You are the truth!" by a very powerful man who stands on a couch to show you how much he means it. You feel electric, and it makes your heart soar. He makes you big, beautiful promises that don't come true. You learn quickly that people say things they don't mean. You quietly harden yourself toward the business and build up your armor.

You'll call your first major-label record *Little Voice* to help you remember to listen to yourself. You only sort of get the message. You are going to muddle through the best you can, and this period of time will launch you onto a roller-coaster ride that will fill you up more than you could ever imagine and then empty out your bones.

You hate your body again. You have to take photographs to use in promotional materials and feel exposed. The girl who photographs you at the studio is so unbelievably beautiful you are embarrassed to have your own face. There is a growing team of people critiquing your image, and it makes you feel violently angry, and you learn to sit on that fire. Their comments on your appearance will be dressed up in kid-glove phrases like, "This look is more flattering," and, "That dress is slimming," and your face will burn hot. You'll only take some of their advice, pretending to be confident in your choices because you are also going to be your most stubborn self in these next few years. I'm glad about that now.

You are defending some unnamed territory inside of you that houses what's true. It exhausts you and burns you out.

You are convinced there are right and wrong answers to all of the questions in front of you, and the pressure is suffocating. You sit alone outside the Sony Tower in busy, bustling midtown Manhattan after a meeting for album artwork where you didn't know what you wanted. After hobbling meekly through the meeting you just sat and cried on the curb until a kind stranger put his hand on your shoulder and said everything was going to be okay. You smiled at this kind person and thanked him but didn't believe him.

He was right.

You are beautiful.

You are overwhelmed and haven't learned to be your own friend through this yet. You will. Your fear of jumping without a net is so valid, and the trick that you haven't learned yet is that that's life, always and everywhere. There are no nets. Life is a big, long free fall, and the sooner you can embrace what is beautiful about that, the sooner you will start to enjoy the ride. You won't really get this for a while, though. Sorry, sister.

You don't feel your own power at all right now, and I understand. Yours is not the kind that wants to announce itself. It is slow and quiet and tucks in behind things waiting to be discovered. Some people have power that is thick and neon-colored and races around the room making sure everyone pays attention. It's fascinating but it's not yours. You are learning how to hold yourself up and believe in the strength of your own conviction. That is not an easy thing to do, and you are doing the best you can. Keep going. I'm very proud of you.

Love,
Sara

Dear Sara,

You are sitting in your hotel room in Sydney, Australia, and feel like you should have your shit together by now. You don't. Overwhelmed with travel and the stress of your job, you have become increasingly anxious, dreading feeling out of control. One way this is manifesting itself is an irrational fear of leaving your hotel room alone, because you believe you'll get lost and not be able to find your way back.

You have written in your journal:

I'm in that fear place again. I feel messy inside. I feel undisciplined and angry and tired. I feel less than.

You buy yourself a book titled *Feel the Fear and Do It Anyway* and you're embarrassed to read it in public, but it helps you make a decision to try and break out of some of your patterns. You eat lunch alone in a café across the street from the hotel and are proud of yourself. You also feel pathetic.

You are on your way to volunteer with an organization called All Hands Volunteers in Ofunato, Japan, after the tsunami. That trip will remind you that we are all very, very small beings who simply have to figure out a way to cope with feeling powerless sometimes. You will be awed and inspired by the people who turn that powerlessness into the power of service.

You will see mountains of debris and thousands of people's belongings that belong nowhere anymore. It's backbreaking work, and your band and crew are all by your side, yet again showing the world their ferocious hearts. It's a deeply soulful place and fills you with gratitude. You will be given Coca-Cola and hot miso soup by an elderly Japanese couple who want to thank your muddy, sweaty, motley team for clearing out the gutters in front of their building. They have nothing. And it means everything.

You are facing a summer of touring, opening for the band Sugarland. The audiences are polite and warm, but you are on borrowed time from the headliner and you can read that in the energy of the crowd. You become insecure about your worth onstage. In Indianapolis, the stage will collapse about twenty minutes after your set. It is bone-chilling and surreal and infinitely tragic. Seven people from the audience will be killed and many more injured. One of the men who dies is a security guard who danced to your music at your sound check. He had a round face, a trim gray beard, and a kind smile. It is devastating, and you will carry that with you for the rest of your life.

You are about to agree to be a judge on a TV singing-competition show that will be the reason you decide to find a therapist again. She will end up being someone extremely important in your life. You will exhaust yourself flying back and forth to shoot the show during the week and then meet up with the tour wherever it is to perform shows on the weekends. It's too much, and it breaks you down.

You will be slapped with your own self-image issues again.

You will be asked to send pictures of yourself at your wardrobe fittings in different dresses for the producers to sift through and decide which ones you are allowed to wear. You will have to do this three different times, because they don't like anything that you choose for yourself. They will put racks of bedazzled dresses in your trailer. It's humiliating and degrading. Executives involved with the show will have meetings outside your trailer about how they aren't happy with the way you look. They'll say you aren't wearing enough flashy jewelry, and that you don't have enough makeup on. You need more hair extensions, and your lipstick should be brighter. Your dresses aren't glamorous enough and you need to be sexier. They'll ping-pong their bullshit to one another in their little huddle two feet from your door and you'll watch through the window and feel numb. Three of them will be women, and you will find that equal parts heartbreaking and infuriating. It brings up a lot of the body issues that you have worked really hard to undo, and you feel manipulated and paralyzed at your own lack of control. You want to rage on behalf of girls everywhere and you don't know how. You will end up wearing sparkly dresses that you hate and you will feel like you don't look like yourself. That part is true. The insecurity this causes bleeds into how you carry yourself, and you will suppress your shame and embarrassment until the season is over. You smile to their faces, talk shit behind their backs, and in the end, lie to the press about why you left the show.

You are beautiful.

Fuck 'em.

The kaleidoscope of experiences you have had this year are deeply meaningful and have enhanced your perspective on what actually matters. You have seen firsthand how fleeting and fragile life is, and it has changed your DNA. Your tolerance for bullshit is lessening, and although you are not always graceful with how you fight back, I love that you are a scrappy little lady.

You are bored with the value system you see celebrated around you. "Compromise" is sometimes just manipulation, and you are learning to identify that. You see a need for more people, women especially, to push back against the system that is in place, and you've decided to do more of that. This experience will only turn up the volume on your voice the next time around. Hell yes to this, and go go go.

Love,
Sara

Dear Sara,

You are writing a book. You have just cut your hair and you chose to try out bangs and you think it looks terrible. You feel old. You went through a recent period of seeing yourself as beautiful but that feels far away from you now. You see your skin changing; more wrinkles and more fatigue. You spend more and more money on products that will reverse the thing that we all know cannot be reversed. You look more and more like your parents, and it feels profound somehow. You are seriously struggling to get over a relationship that recently ended. You thought you were going to grow old with him, and you are resisting letting go. You don't believe anyone will ever love you as much as he did. You are throwing yourself into your work. You are feeling uplifted and overwhelmed in equal parts most of the time. You have carved out a place for yourself in an industry that you still don't understand very well, and you don't feel inspired to keep making music in the same way you have before. You don't know what you're going to do with that yet. You feel like writing this book is the hardest thing you have ever done, and you're certain that people will think you're stupid, or not funny, or saccharine, or too precious, or a million other adjectives describing a negative experience. You have a loud voice inside yourself that is telling you that you aren't good enough and aren't pretty enough and aren't smart enough ... AND YOU TOTALLY SEE WHAT'S HAPPENING HERE, DON'T YOU?

You are beautiful.

I am your friend and I wouldn't lie to you. This will be a conversation you can count on having with yourself forever and ever, so get comfy. There are always going to be reasons to doubt your own worth; the question is, how far do you allow yourself to go down that road before you look up and realize that, just like that girl in the ruby-red slippers, you had the power to come home all along?

Things evolve into other things. Emotions do the same. Forever. Your best ally in all of these shifting seas is your faith in the fact that you are exactly where you are supposed to be. Stay put. Stay soft. Stay gentle and kind. Listen to your instincts. Meditate. Pray. Laugh as much as humanly possible. Pain is okay too. Say thank you for all of it. Feel proud that you have spent most of your life's energy on cultivating a strong connection to your own soul and the will of your heart. It is leading you somewhere deeply satisfying but never perfect. Observe what is painful right now and see if you can stay courageous enough to share it wholly and honestly. Invite it into your house and be a good student. You are a patchwork quilt of all of these past selves, all these wounded little girls, and they are all here too, listening in some form or another. You have grown into someone I am very proud of, and though I wish I could give you the gift of knowing we won't ever need to have this conversation again . . . that's not really the point, and probably not true.

The work is learning to love whatever it is, so for now let's do that, shall we?

I love you, my beautiful girl, and I hope that's enough.

Love,
Sara

RED

CHAPTER
five

Red

I'm fading in and out
What are you supposed to do, save me now?
From all of this danger, you don't know how
And I'll find my way out
When I'm in the Red
Listening to strangers inside my head
The darkening angels beneath the bed
I still see everything you said
In crimson and Red.

RED

THE DAY I MET Joni Mitchell was as profound an experience as I have ever had in my life. Now, I will start by saying I've never actually *met* Joni Mitchell, but I was introduced to her music by a total stranger in a tiny music school I stumbled upon in the streets of Italy, in the middle of a nervous breakdown.

I spent the whole of my junior year of college in Bologna, Italy, in an exchange program, studying Italian language, literature, and how many pizzas I could eat in one sitting. (At least two.) My life in Italy was a complicated, yearlong exploration of self-discovery. I was hunting myself down while in the context of a completely foreign world. Some of it was euphoric. Some of it was devastating. All of it was wildly important to shaping me as a human.

HIGHLIGHTS:

I ate the fooooooooooooood.

In Italy, it's totally acceptable for a person to eat an entire pizza alone in one sitting and, well, that's just outstanding. Italy, you are the granter of wishes. My obsession with Italian food only grew after my year abroad, partly because of the food in Bologna. The city is in the heart of a northern region of Italy called Emilia-Romagna, and is best known for the richness of its cuisine. Hearty, rustic food like meaty Bolognese sauce, long blonde noodles called tagliatelle, and the delicious and fatty mortadella (the Italian bologna) are just a few of the things that were available anytime, anywhere, and were best when washed down with a pizza. I came to know that truly authentic Italian food is actually quite simple, made with a few high-quality ingredients, patience, and plenty of good olive oil. It was hard to find a bad meal, and I didn't find too many, clearly, as evidenced by the twenty pounds I gained while I lived there, which might be more of a "lowlight" kinda thing.

I went to Rome.

I have never been somewhere new that left such an immediate impression. So much so, that during a long walk along the sloped banks of the wide river through the center of the city, I convinced myself that in a past life I was a Roman girl. I visited a few different times over the year, and each time fell deeper in love with the grandeur and muscle of that sprawling city. Even its rough edges were inviting. I once stayed in a youth hostel near the train station that reminded me of the dark, dilapidated house in *Fight Club.* I briefly thought my friend and I might actually die at the hands of the madman with peroxide-blond hair, who was living in one of the rooms of the hostel. He mumbled things under his breath like, "Keep me away from that window!!" while we tried not to make direct eye contact. He turned out to be a harmless man named Ron, who called every woman "flower" while singing original songs he wrote about forest animals. Rome was full of surprise and wonder like that. It loomed up, first like a fortress, but then eventually softened into a rambling stone maze of history and art and ruin and light. Before I left the hostel, I was kissed passionately by a quiet Roman boy with dimples in a broom closet, and the next day he presented me with a handmade drawing of a delicate alien flower inspired by me. Rome is magnificent.

I learned to speak Italian.

Not perfectly, mind you, but pretty damn well. I could walk into a shop and ask for exactly what I wanted without the hot flash of panic that used to accompany that exchange. I still had the vocabulary of a slow-learning four-year-old, but I was proud of myself and gained confidence in my ability to communicate. Eventually, something just clicked, and even though I was still speaking in fairly simple terms, I stopped having to translate every word from English to Italian in my mind before I spoke. There was a newfound ease and fluidity with my speech, like I was a rusty bicycle chain that had finally clicked into a higher, smoother gear. I spent entire evenings around a dinner table with new university friends, clinking glasses of cheap red table wine, speaking only Italian, and came away from those nights full of something even more satisfying than the pasta and tiramisu.

LOWLIGHTS:

Most of the American TV shows are overdubbed with Italian voices.

IT'S FUCKING ANNOYING. *Friends. The Simpsons. Seinfeld.* All of them. The bottom line is, I don't want to *watch* Elaine push Jerry and say, "Get OUT!!!" but *hear* "VAI VIA!!!" in the voice of some woman who is not Julia Louis-Dreyfus. I don't want Phoebe to be in the Central Perk coffee shop playing her guitar, singing Smelly Cat, but have to settle for some rough translation of it that ends up being Cat Stinking sung by the Italian Kathleen Turner. In my time away from home, I craved certain creature comforts like peanut butter (which they don't sell anywhere), large coffees in to-go cups (not a chance in hell), and George Costanza in his own voice. I know this sounds trivial, but this one hit me where it hurt, in my TV bone.

I hated being a woman sometimes.

At first I didn't see or feel a problem with the constant chatter from men; in fact, I enjoyed getting some attention, and much of it seemed innocuous. "*Ciao bella*" from a stranger as you walk by isn't particularly offensive, but it starts to grate on your nerves after a year of hearing it and seeing it anywhere and everywhere. You start to question whether or not it's "fair" for a man to get to say whatever he thinks about you simply because you have boobs and a vagina. The catcalling was constant, and most of the time, it was more direct and less innocent. My American roommate got hit on at a dance club and then got her hair yanked when she refused to dance with one particular guy. I shocked myself when I grabbed the collar of his shirt and shoved him to the ground and got us all kicked out of the bar. I got my crotch grabbed, standing in a crowd at a concert, by some mystery hand that snaked out from somewhere and then disappeared. It left me feeling the sickening buzz of having been violated without any possibility of recourse.

I also noticed that commenting on and critiquing a woman's physical appearance was fair game for regular old conversation. It was everyday chitchat like, "Can I pour you a coffee? You got fatter, I think. How's your mom?" I saw this for the first time when my grumpy, short, fat Italian roommate (with a portrait of Stalin over his bed, if that tells you anything) told my stick-thin, gentle, beautiful, bookish roommate that she had gained weight over the holiday break as if he had been discussing the weather. She just sheepishly laughed and agreed that she should skip some meals. I scowled at his dumpy awfulness, finished my plate of pasta, and wondered what I would say if I was ever put in that situation.

I got to answer my own question at the end of the year, when I sat down with my History of Photography professor for the final oral exam and the first thing he said was, *"Sei un po'ingrassata, eh?"* (You've gained a little weight, huh?)

The shock of such a statement took me by surprise, and it stung. Regrettably, I only laughed uncomfortably and told him, "Yeah, I really liked the food," because I didn't know what tense to use to tell him he was a shithead in Italian.

I was desperately lonely.

Even at my best, I still only spoke rudimentary Italian. There's only so much of yourself that gets expressed in "ONE HAM SANDWICH PLEASE!" and "I AM STUDENT! I STUDY THE COMMUNICATIONS! I EAT THREE PIZZA TODAY!" In any given situation I could only express a fraction of what my brain was thinking or feeling, and it felt like I was projecting a dulled sense of my own personality. Because of my limitations with the language, I had very little nuance. No humor. No bite. It's maddening to be in a conversation wanting to show someone who you are, while expressing yourself like a child. It kept me feeling isolated from my Italian friends and leaning hard on my American ones, who were great, but difficult in their own ways. I had fiery friendships that were fraught with unnecessary drama, and by the sheer nature of the study program's design, everything felt temporary. One year of all this craziness and then we'd all go back to our "real" lives. I was living in a strange limbo world, not totally connecting to what was immediately around me, but still incredibly far from what I would be going home to.

I couldn't shake this feeling that we were all in suspended animation during our year in Italy. It didn't matter what I did, because my actual life was waiting for me at home. I experimented with things I had never done before, feeling like it was justified because I was in an alternate universe. I made stupid, rash decisions and let myself off my own leash for a while. It was my own personal *Rumspringa*. I was *exactly* like an Amish teenager on a free pass to explore the world outside my community. (Note to self: Find better metaphor *before* book goes to print.)

I started smoking. I got my eyebrow pierced. I barely went to class. I asked for rides on scooters with random dudes late at night. I drank many drinks many times. I took ecstasy that didn't work at a dance club and everyone else felt gypped and I felt relieved.

In trying to find my footing I lost my grip.

One night I smoked weed with my two American girl-friends on my couch, watching a documentary about Bob Marley. The night started out breezy. We were laughing, making dinner together, and I felt light and warm, the way marijuana and Bob Marley are theoretically supposed to make you feel. Then I felt a shift, and the sensation turned a corner into something colder and darker. I started to hear my internal monologue at a screaming volume, and it was telling me I was crazy. I left the girls in the living room without telling them what was going on and went to lie down in the little twin bed of my peach-colored bedroom. I put on Fiona Apple's *Tidal*, one of my favorite records, and the room was spinning around me as she sang Sullen Girl. I frantically wrote in my journal, trying to keep up with how fast my thoughts were coming, but the whole act of it scared me further. I felt out of control.

It wasn't just too much marijuana: it was a kind of home-sickness, but not for my life in LA or anything that had come before. I craved some sense of knowledge that I was going to be all right out here in the world, all by myself.

The day that followed was terrible. My emotional hang-over was thick and thorny and I felt antsy, wanting to crawl out of my own skin. I had hoped I would sleep off those weird, crazy feelings and wake up "normal," but my melancholy was everywhere and I couldn't pretend otherwise. I sat in an Internet café and wrote again in my journal about how heavy the feelings were, waiting for something to lift, but I had been introduced to what would become a leading char-acter in my life. The melancholy that cracked open that night would eventually become something I'm deeply fond of, but we never know which monsters under the bed will become our friends, do we?

I took a morning walk that led me into the belly of a tall Catholic cathedral, where I asked for God's help on my knees from one of the empty wooden pews. *Please, God, guide me toward something that feels like home.* I walked out of the massive church and its medieval arched doors, back to my apartment, and sent out my version of the bat signal. I called my dad. Through my tears I told him that I was having a really hard time and that I thought I needed him to send me my key-board immediately. I don't know why *that* was my solution in the moment, but it just was. A smarter, savvier person might have noticed that they actually sell keyboards in Italy, but BACK OFF, I'M HAVING A CRISIS!!!!! Aside from singing

At Merry Melodies Music School
in Bologna, Italy, 2001

a couple of times in a restaurant that belonged to friends, I wasn't involved in anything music related, and I hadn't been writing at all for the months I had already spent in Italy. The black and white keys of my shitty little keyboard were the only things I could think of that felt like a safe place to go. My darling father took it to FedEx that very morning, and I was at least a little bit relieved to know it was on its way. I was less relieved to know that, with shipping and taxes, it was going to cost us around six hundred dollars. Merry Christmas, FedEx.

The sky took its cue from my stormy mood and opened up with torrential rains as I arrived home to my little apartment. Being inside felt worse than being wet, so after I hung up with my dad, I gathered my Walkman (yep . . .) and an umbrella and headed out in search of something I hadn't identified yet. A few doors down from the entrance to the building was a large commercial music shop. I absentmindedly made that my first stop. They had big walls of books of sheet music and racks of CDs in those gigantic useless plastic bricks they used to come in, and a small selection of musical instruments. I walked past the headphones, guitars, small keyboards, and amplifiers straight to the man behind the counter. I thought I could inquire about piano lessons maybe, or practice rooms, but I didn't really know. I was fumbling over the words themselves, as well as tears so fresh they could begin again at any second, but managed to ask about piano lessons. This particular store didn't offer them, but the man was kind and spoke slowly and said there was a small music school relatively close to our neighborhood. I had a destination now, at least.

This was before we held phone-shaped maps in our hands at all times, so it felt more like a treasure hunt than anything else. I darted between the rain and the porticos, the big overhangs that are on practically every building in Bologna, and after some time searching down small streets, I saw the tiny white sign that said MERRY MELODIES. The roll-down metal gate was mostly closed, but there was light coming through the window from a back room. I rang the bell.

A tall man with salt-and-pepper hair and a smile came to the door, raised the gate, and hurried me inside out of the rain. He spoke to me in Italian, saying that the shop was closed for the day and the piano teacher wasn't there, so I would have to come back another time. As I stuttered through thanking him for letting me in, my unrefined Italian tipped him off, and he immediately broke into English.

I would come to learn many things about Michael Bruscia in a very short amount of time. That day in the lobby, I learned he was an American music teacher who had been living in Bologna for twenty-plus years, thus giving him an endearing hodgepodge mash-up vocabulary and pronunciation. He says things like "Cal-ee-*for*-nee-yuh" and "That's just fantastico!!" He is from Wisconsin, which he visits every three years, and has a son named Daniele who is also very musical. He moved to Bologna after marrying his Italian wife, and he conducts a jazz orchestra called Born to Swing in addition to giving saxophone lessons and running the studio. I would eventually learn that Michael argues passionately about Bob Dylan's canon of work. He can drink anybody under the table with great cheer, as I imagine Santa Claus might if he were a drinker, and best of all, he has an enthusiasm for life that makes you question your own tendency to think anything *isn't* amazing.

He was genuine and warm, and so curious about my being in Bologna, and we went very quickly from talking about the prospect of piano lessons to discussing life in Italy as an American. We spoke about music and why I felt compelled to take lessons. I told him I was a singer and a beginning songwriter and he immediately invited me to share something I had written. I was hesitant, but he was so sure that it would be wonderful that I kind of wanted to see for myself. He ushered me into the small, cluttered lesson room adjacent to the tiny lobby entrance. Lit by an old side-table lamp, the room had an upright piano, stacks of sheet-music books, a couple of chairs, and an old record player in the corner. I sat down at the piano and scanned my brain for anything I could play by heart, which was not much. I nervously settled on one of my original songs, Everyday Stranger, and after I finished, Michael applauded and begged for another song. I felt proud. I played Gravity, which was one of the other songs in my repertoire. He showered me with compliments and *fantasticos* and I blushed and felt special and good and deeply happy for the first time in a long time.

Michael asked me if I knew the album *Blue*, by Joni Mitchell. Of course I had heard her name, but I had to admit that I wasn't familiar with her music. I had just recently ended a phase of my life where I listened almost exclusively to *NSync and Britney Spears, but I omitted that part. He felt a need to share a particular song with me. The crackle of the vinyl began, then the jangly chords of the dulcimer, and then I heard the pure arrow of Joni's voice pierce the instrumentation, and something in me. The song he played was "California."

And I cried.

Silently, facing away from Michael, staring at the keys of the piano. Her words bloomed into vivid pictures in my mind, and her message, delivered by way of that delicate, haunting soprano, made my heart swell. I felt like somebody had thrown me a rope. The song made peace with living between two worlds, and I somehow felt understood and comforted immediately (in spite of not knowing what a "sunset pig" was). I felt relieved listening to her capture the rapture and mystery of a foreign place and, in the same breath, ache for a sense of home. It was so pure. I told Michael how homesick I was. How I missed a sense of myself. He understood completely. Even for someone who had long since made a very happy life in that Italian world, he could relate to the feeling of missing where you come from, at the same time knowing that you can never really go back.

Michael and I listened through that song and a few others off of her masterpiece album, *Blue*, and I immediately felt an urge to make my own experiences sing like that. In my own way, of course, I could try and build songs that might serve as monuments to my own private revelations, and make them into something that wouldn't terrify, but enlighten me. Teach me. Release me, too. In that moment, I wanted to go straight to my piano and unravel the mess of emotion and anxiety inside me and make it into something beautiful. It felt like pieces of some puzzle had clicked into place, and music was the soul center of it all. Songwriting wasn't a hobby. It was my lifeline.

Michael and I spoke for about an hour and I left lighter, with a sense of direction. He invited me to come back the following week, and I did. I took a couple of piano lessons, but after Michael suggested I come sing some songs with his

*On stage at Ca' Bianca
in Milan, December 2000*

jazz orchestra, I focused only on that. He made me mixtapes
of songs to learn by some of the greatest women in jazz. I got
to know Ella Fitzgerald, Sarah Vaughan, and Billie Holiday.
I started singing standards with Born to Swing on a regular
basis, and we played at clubs, weddings, parties, community
events, and even a jazz club in Milan called Ca' Bianca. At
the end of the performance, the owner of the club presented
me with a bouquet of flowers and we took photographs while
the audience cheered like I was somebody. My picture was in

the local Milanese paper the next day, and I have to say, that felt pretty fantastico.

My keyboard arrived a week or so after my quest to Merry Melodies, and after a snafu with the voltage of Italian outlets, a certain burning smell, and me again realizing I should have just bought a fucking keyboard in Italy, I got my writing station settled and started pouring my stories into my music. With my keyboard next to my bed I felt less alone, like I had a friend that wouldn't leave my side. I wrote the song Red in that same peach-colored bedroom where I thought I was losing my mind. It spoke to my recent realization that I felt out of bounds and couldn't depend on my parents or my past to save me, but that was okay. I felt whole again when I wrote the lyric "How you love is who you are." It sounded like me. I gained a little patience with the uncertainty swirling around me and, through writing about my experience, found my way back to something inside myself that I recognized. I surrendered more fully to what was out of my control and started feeling less sorry for myself, which continue to be two of the fastest and most effective ways to change my perspective.

It's been fifteen years since I lived in that apartment in Bologna, looking down over the crowded roundabout filled with mopeds and tiny Italian cars. I have lost touch with most of my roommates and friends from that time, but I still get a call from Michael Bruscia every three years when he visits Wisconsin. I look forward to that phone call, because in addition to the general wave of nostalgia for what ended up being a very rich and meaningful time in my life, it reminds me of that day in the rain, when he introduced me to Joni. I have since shed the extra pounds and most of my Italian vocabulary, but retained a lot of what I learned in Italy. Among the many things I took away:

1. The Italian post office can close any time it wants to, for any reason at all.
2. Cappuccinos are not for after dinner. Espressos are.
3. Italy *is* beauty.
4. How you love is who you are.
5. My soul is a songwriter.

MANY
the
MILES

CHAPTER
six

many the miles

There's too many things I haven't
done yet
There's too many sun sets I haven't seen
you can't waste the day wishing it'd slow down
you would have thought by now
    I'd have learned something

I made up my mind when I was a young girl
I've been given this one world
  I won't worry it away
  But now and again I lose sight of the good life
I get stuck in a low light
        But then LOVE comes in.
How far do I have to go to get to you?
    Many the miles.
      Many the miles
How far do I have to go to get to you?
Many the miles
  But send me the miles and I'll be happy to
    follow you, love.

MANY THE MILES

———

HAVE SPENT MANY MONTHS of my life on the road. It's one of my favorite parts about my job, because I get to see the world through the lens of sharing music, and there is nothing I have found that is more gratifying. I'll never forget the moment I looked up at the tiers of the audience—lit up—of my sold-out show at Radio City Music Hall. I was wearing a leather tank top and a tutu, and dedicated The Way You Look Tonight to my dad, who stood in the audience. I watched a sea of college kids fist-pump to a song about finding your soul mate, merely because I asked them to. I have looked across the top of my piano onstage while Sir Elton John sang Gravity and Carole

King sang Brave. I have hugged Stevie Wonder, and I can tell you for a fact that he's squishy. The memories fold into each other like paint on a colossal canvas. It's an elaborate, repeating sequence of morning coffees and late-night bourbons, and everything that happens in between. It is a beautiful blur.

The stage is like the Wild West: anything can happen, and usually does. This has been the single greatest teacher I have encountered in my life in helping me learn to stay flexible and roll with the punches. For example, on a solo tour in Austin, Texas, the power to the main speakers might short-circuit for several minutes in the middle of a show. Instead of panicking, this is a good time to break out into Part of Your World, from *The Little Mermaid*. You might also try crowd-surfing. Or, perhaps in St. Louis, the sound of the piano might suddenly disappear as you start playing your solo encore song. Instead of getting angry at the technical malfunction, you might, instead, consider talking to the audience about the first time you got your period. The unpredictability of live performance has encouraged me to flex my own ability to stay playful. It's a metaphor for the bigger picture too, as many times life doesn't follow the rules. This reminder is part of what makes performance so magical and keeps me coming back for more.

Despite the overall blur of touring, there are all kinds of moments that remain distinct and intact. In August 2013, I got an invitation to sing my song Brave with Taylor Swift at her show in Los Angeles. Besides a flattering invite, this was an opportunity to become "Super Auntie" to my two young nieces, who I'm incessantly trying to convince of my coolness. At our afternoon rehearsal at the arena, I learned I would be entering the stage from the elevator platform at the top of a giant staircase. I had never entered any kind of room from an elevator platform, so this simultaneously made me feel nervous and like a Power Ranger. After sound check, my family and I got ready for the show in my dressing room and then headed out to our seats to watch Taylor. She danced and sang and bubbled over onstage like pink champagne. My nieces were in heaven.

It was then time for me to go backstage to get my in-ear monitors on. The stage manager escorted me to the back of the stage and I stood on the giant metal platform, waiting for my introduction. My heart was racing. I heard the drum introduction of Brave begin and then the ground beneath me started rising upward. Taylor called out my name on the microphone and then . . .

Nothing.

I couldn't hear ANYTHING but the deafening roar of thousands of tweenage apocalyptic screams. I frantically listened for any music at all. I knew the drums had started, but literally no other sounds could pierce the wall of "woo." I couldn't hear the beginning notes of the piano over the crowd, so I ripped out my earpiece to try and hear the speaker system of the venue at least. No good. All I could hear was even louder girl-euphoria. It was time to start singing, so I basically just picked a note out of thin air. I could immediately feel in my throat muscles that it was the wrong one, and I'll never forget the panicked look on the music director's face on the side of the stage that just said, "Noooooooooooooooooooooo!!" I tried a bunch of other wrong notes for the whole first verse but finally hunted down the right ones by the chorus. I was mortified, but I couldn't do anything except keep singing for the fans cheering us on. I smiled and danced with Taylor at the end of the catwalk and pretended everything was fine. We got through the song, she hugged me, and I came offstage and felt awful.

I felt like I had embarrassed myself at a moment when I'd had something to prove. It was like getting called up to play with the "big boys" (or girls!!) and I felt like I hadn't been able to hold my own. I was caught up in the drama of feeling exposed, until Taylor lightened my load. After the show, she came into my dressing room and was graceful and sparkly and complimentary and only *celebrated* our performance. It was almost like saying, "Yeah, sure, that *one* part was whatever, but the *rest* of it was so good!" She shared a story about a similar situation she'd had on an even bigger stage with even bigger artists, and by doing so, let the air out of my mistake. By treating the mistake with so little weight, it actually became weightless. It was a learning moment for me, and I took note, and will put that into practice again.

The people who see the good, the bad, and the ugly up close and personal are the members of my touring family; my band mates and crew members who have been there every step of the way. The names and faces have changed a few times over the years, but the bonds that form are remarkable. Some of these folks were my closest confidants during the time when my life changed the most dramatically, around the release of my first record in 2007. They were in the trenches with me,

Javier Dunn (left), Daniel Rhine, myself,
Josh Day, and Eric Robinson in Eureka, 2010

carrying keyboards and cajóns and acoustic guitars into conference rooms at radio stations, begging people to come out to
our shows. Over the next few years, we were lucky enough to
witness vans and trailers turn into buses, and dirty little rock
clubs turn into quaint little theaters and then giant stadiums.
All of our lives changed a lot during that time. My little family.
You don't forget that.

Javier Dunn played guitar beside me for many years and
was my heart for so long. I fell in love with him alongside making the music, and he held my hand through many of my hard-

est moments by inviting me to search myself for the answers, and spent almost a decade with me in music. Fiercely independent and funny as hell, he was an essential ingredient to the alchemy of our life on the road, and my life in general.

I met Josh Day when he covered a gig for another drummer in 2003, and after that first show together, he sat behind the drum set with me for close to ten years. He is my life-loving Southern Leo, bighearted and supremely sensitive, and we were like brother and sister. We still are. We fight like it sometimes, but love each other through it all, and over the years he lifted my music (and our spirits) with his steady hands and, many times, a jar of moonshine.

Daniel Rhine was the bass player who finally fit. I went through about eleven different bass players until Dan finally slid into place seamlessly as if he'd always been there. He is steady and quiet, but can be rowdy when you least expect it. He reads books about John Adams FOR FUN and likes long walks, Scrabble, beer, and Javi's jokes. He elevated the music, made me smile, and also has a large head, which he won't mind me mentioning here. Hi, Dan.

Some folks were with me for years, some for only a short time (for lots of colorful reasons). One crew member tried to crawl inside of the overhead compartments on the bus when he got drunk. Another got high in Amsterdam before a show and left his post at the side of the stage during the show because he "got hungry." Most added something unique and important to the tour, and it's just the way life works; even the best things don't last forever. Sometimes the change is of our choosing and some-

times it's not, but touring reminds me everything is always in motion. Good stuff gets worse and bad stuff gets better, so you're better off to spend a little time making friends with all of it.

Just as being onstage is unpredictable, anything can happen behind the scenes, and usually does, so choosing good

Daniel Rhine (left), Javier Dunn, and me at the Ryman Auditorium in Nashville, October 9, 2010

people to share the road with is essential. A sense of humor and a good attitude are always helpful along the way. We are on the front lines of each other's lives with only a few feet between us, on a bus, for weeks and sometimes months on end. We are together in airports and truck stops and bus lounges for hours and hours. We can't help but swap hearts, because sometimes the displaced feeling that comes with constant motion breeds a particular brand of honesty. Or playfulness. Or boredom. Or sometimes you order an assortment of 250 knives and two Samurai swords from a middle-of-the night infomercial and send them to your tour manager's house, because vodka. (Sorry about that, Trey.)

During our summer tour of 2014, on the Little Black Dress tour, our bus broke down incessantly. We logged twenty-two different breakdowns and/or issues with the bus in a six-week stretch. This unfortunate situation brought most of us to our breaking point. My poor tour manager and bus driver spent more hours dealing with this than anyone else, but everybody felt the strain of the constant breakdowns. It happened so often, it prevented us from sleeping, and the extra travel was hard on our bodies and our morale. I have to admit that and my humor ran out toward the end of the tour, and made me hate just about everything. I wouldn't have been able to handle the stress of that without my band and crew who all pooled together to make it work. Chris Morrissey, my musical director, favorite comedian, and one of the best decisions I ever made, remembers our bus:

—

CHRIS MORRISSEY
BASS/MUSICAL DIRECTOR

We were told that this bus was the bee's knees. It *was* the bee's knees in a beauty contest. In the getting-us-to-the-next-gig contest, it was some other kind of knees. Former-running-back knees. We learned this the hard way. Repeatedly.

I don't remember the first time we broke down. I remember a few in the middle. One featured being rescued somewhere in the Deep South by a tiny school bus. We all still found it funny at that point, laughing our un-slept asses off in that little thing. We waited at a truck stop and ate hospital-grade breakfast in our sweatpants, and when we climbed back onto the bus, we all had gifts from Sara. Mine was a knife that had JOHN written on it that I'm currently using to carve this essay.

But the last breakdown takes the cake. It started when we were jarred awake by the now familiar death rattle. The muffled fury of the driver barely audible through two doors, but audible enough. Our tour manager, CB, charged forward to draw up a battle plan. iPhones popped to life behind bunk curtains as we all saw where our Google map pin was. We were heading to San Diego, which by all accounts was eight hours away. It looked to me like we were eight hours from anything but cooked dirt.

When I emerged into the front lounge, Sara was making mimosas with a furrowed brow. "We're all gonna die out here," she said. Okay, she didn't really say that, but what she did say was almost as shocking. "We're looking into chartering a plane."

"That sounds cheap," I said back. The furrow didn't budge. We took our mimosas outside and, from the side of I-5 in central California, all eight of us began throwing dirt clods at this piece-of-shit bus. We were snapping pictures and posting. I tried to get #fuckthisbus to trend, but it didn't really catch on. News came in that we had indeed chartered a plane to San Diego from the nearest airstrip (which was a sad piece of asphalt IN THE MIDDLE OF NOWHERE). We waited for our ride for a long time as the air in the dead bus became increasingly like the air in the 105-degree desert, and the mimosas were wearing off. Finally it came, and it was one of those party limos that you would go to prom in if your prom was in suburban Minneapolis. We filed out and straight onto a tiny plane and met the pilot, who looked pilotey enough, and, surrounded by suitcases in the tiny cabin, we flew very quietly to San Diego.

I've never given birth, but I have a few tattoos, and I've heard that they're similar: your brain tricks you into not remembering how traumatic the experience can feel so it lives in your mind as something you might want to do again. Maybe I'm tricked, but I remember a lot of smiling.

I remember a lot of smiling too. From my OG family to my Little Black Dress tour peeps, it's been a wild ride of laughing and loving, and I am a better human because they were there.

The best part of being on tour by far is getting to know my

Chris Morrissey (left), Misty Boyce, Rich Hinman,
Claire Indie, myself, Cara Fox, and Steve Goold
backstage at Radio City Music Hall, 2013

fans. They have held me up (crowd-surfing and otherwise) over the years, and their belief in what I do makes me believe in it too. They make me scrapbooks of letters and pictures and wait for hours to only maybe get to say hello. They want to share their music or share their story, and I wish I had all the time in the world to make each and every one of them feel seen. They want to tell me that I make a difference. Sometimes I don't know how to process how that feels. It makes me feel very big and very small at the same time. I know that without them, this business is a meaningless machine, and I don't think they will ever know how much they've given me.

During my Kaleidoscope Heart tour in 2010, a girl passed a gift bag to me over the heads of a crowd at a small radio event in Minneapolis. I didn't see where the bag had come from initially, but spotted the girl waving her hand to me as I picked up the bag and exited the stage at the end of the show. When I got back to my dressing room I looked inside. It was a carved wooden kaleidoscope in the shape of a heart, and it was gorgeous. With it was a letter in which this girl shared that she had been struggling with depression for many years. She had recently come to the conclusion that it was time to take her own life. But, by the grace of God, the act itself was interrupted by a song of mine that came on the radio called Hold My Heart. Something in the music connected to her in that moment and stopped her from doing the unthinkable. She changed her mind. She told me her story in a letter instead, and as I read her words, I was moved to tears. The profundity of that kind of sadness, coupled with the power of music, was overwhelming.

I wrote her a letter the next day and encouraged her to get professional help and shared a number for a suicide hotline as well as mental health support resources. I could tell from her letter that she was an extremely gifted writer, and I encouraged her to tell her story in writing. We have stayed in touch over the years, and it was a proud moment to write to her once again, as I finished this essay, and ask her to tell her story in writing again.

JESSICA VICKER

In the middle of the night on September 27, 2010, Sara's lyrics to Hold My Heart played through my speakers and saved my life, as that was the day that I had planned would be my last due to the debilitating symptoms of major depressive disorder that had paralyzed me for so long. Two short months later, on November 2, 2010, I was able to tell her my story in the form of a letter I had written.

April 9, 2011, will probably always be my fondest memory of Sara, as that was the first day we were able to meet in person. Thanks to all of the right stars aligning at the right time, the scribbled note I gave to the man at the ticket booth telling Sara I would be in the crowd that night made it into her hands! I have forgotten many of the things that we said to each other that night, but I will never forget the way she made me feel. It's the same way I always feel whenever I listen to her music—safe, powerful, and of course BRAVE, all feelings that my illness had robbed me of for so long. I made a promise to her that night that has been in the back of my mind, guiding my thoughts and actions every day since. She made me "pinky promise" that no matter what was to come throughout the rest of my recovery, I would continue to "choose to fight the good fight" and would never allow myself to forget my own strength.

Today, I am very proud to say that I have kept that promise. As Sara's fans, none of us experience her music the same way, but the message that is communicated is overwhelmingly the same: that we are here for a purpose, we're all stronger than we know, and we're all meant to leave a legacy. I hope one day the legacy I leave will be similar to Sara's, that I will be able to have touched and maybe even saved some lives through my work as a mental health practitioner, where I am able to share my recovery story with others.

———

Jessica was a gift to me. All my fans are. The part of me that comes to life in front of them is my most powerful, confident, whole, courageous self. My fans see things in me that I am not always able to see. They are always reminding me, in gorgeous little ways, that connection is the most important part of all of this. Yet again, a soulful lesson from the road.

On the final night of my tour for *The Blessed Unrest*, we played the Greek Theater in Berkeley, California. Visually it's an impressive venue, set back beneath tall evergreens, with high raked seats made of what looks like marble. It makes you feel like you're playing on the stage at the Colosseum in Rome, with more trees and fewer gladiators. The final song of the night was a song called Satellite Call. I wrote it inspired by stories like Jessica's, for my fans who have shared with me over the years their fears of being lost in the world. I closed my eyes while I sang most of the song that night. . . .

This one's for the lonely child
the brokenhearted

the running wild
This was written for the one to blame
The one who believe they are the cause of chaos in
*   everything*

You may find yourself in the dead of night
Lost somewhere out there in that great big beautiful sky
You are all just perfect little satellites
Spinning round and round this broken earthly life

This is so you'll know the sound
Of someone who loves you from the ground
Tonight you're not alone at all
This is me sending out my satellite call

It took my breath away when I opened my eyes to see the entire audience had held up the flashlights on their phones, creating a blanket of thousands of tiny, twinkling, swirling lights, surrounding us. I have seen lots of videos of this happening for other artists onstage, but I can count on one hand the number of times I have experienced it myself. It might seem silly, but it felt like a symbolic exchange. Of being heard and seen. Each little light represented somebody out there who was listening, and collectively, they created a sea of stars. A sea of souls, rather, and I was honored to be among them. It was an enchanted send-off for the evening and for the whole tour, a memory that will make me excited to pack my bags the next time and discover what other magic is waiting out there on the road.

BRAVE

CHAPTER
seven

Brave.

You can be amazing
  You can turn a phrase into a weapon
    or a drug
You can be the outcast
  Or be the backlash of somebody's lack of love
Or you can start speaking up
Nothing's gonna hurt you the way that words do
  When they settle 'neath your skin
Kept on the inside, no sunlight
  Sometimes a shadow wins
But I wonder what would happen if you

  Say what you want to say
    And let the words fall out honestly
I want to see you be brave
  with what you want to say
And let the words fall out honestly
  I want to see you be brave.

  Maybe there's a way out
    of the cage where you live
maybe one of these days you can
  let the light in
  And show me how big your BRAVE is.

BRAVE

BRAVE CAME INTO MY LIFE because of Jack Antonoff, and I met Jack because of Tegan and Sara, and I met Tegan and Sara because of Lilith Fair, which is how I met the Indigo Girls, which is like seeing unicorns up close.

I have been a huge fan of Tegan and Sara for a long time. They are talented, passionate, articulate, outspoken women in music. They've built a massively successful music career and a devoted fan base on super-smart indie rock/pop songs and a unique sound that doesn't resemble that of anyone else in our current musical landscape. (They do, however, resemble each other. Twin joke . . . get it? Never mind.) I was so excited to get to play a show with them in Boston at the 2010 Lilith Fair. My friendship with Sara began backstage after the show, where we learned we could make each other laugh, and sometimes that's all you need to know about a person to know that being friends is a good idea.

The girls were spending some time in LA recording in 2012, and I accepted an invitation from Sara to come by and say hello to them in the studio. It was a warm day, and I walked into Dangerbird studios feeling utterly out of place because that's what Silver Lake, home of the bohemian hipster, does to me. Every store on the block has artisanal "olde" things that I don't know how to use, sold by a beautiful man in suspenders and a mustache that I don't know how to talk to. I was immediately welcomed by the twins and, in their charming, self-effacing way, they reminded me that they never feel cool either, which, now that I think of it, is one of the reasons we became friends in the first place. When really cool people don't know they're cool, it makes them especially appealing.

I heard some of their new music, which was amazing and thoughtful and dreamy and melodic and danceable. I was in the thick of trying to write songs for my own record and making decisions on the direction of the production, feeling overwhelmed. Sara told me about how much fun she'd had in her writing sessions with one of her best friends, Jack Antonoff, whom I had never heard of, but I thought his name sounded regal. Sara suggested I meet him and, if nothing else, she was confident that we would like each other and have good conversation. I would learn later that Jack is good conversation's best friend. She put us in touch via e-mail, and a month or so later, I met him for breakfast in Santa Monica.

I walked up Montana Avenue toward Blue Plate café, one of my favorite little sunny breakfast spots close to an old apartment of mine. Jack lives in New York and was just getting out of a taxi when I walked up, which is completely normal in New York but the equivalent of arriving on horseback in Los Angeles. He spilled out of the backseat of the cab with arms full of bags and a backpack and a white tuxedo in a see-through garment bag, and I immediately loved him. I asked him why he'd brought everything he owned to our breakfast meeting and he laughed and explained he was eventually heading back to the airport to go home that day. The tuxedo was from his performance with his band, FUN., at the MTV Music Video Awards the previous night. I didn't know at the time, but Jack is so humble he would never have offered up that information unless I'd asked.

He had his signature thick, dark-rimmed glasses and close-cut hairstyle, and was wearing a gray sweatshirt with the sleeves cut short, and rolled-up jeans, which made him seem like a young boxer straight out of the '50s. We sat at a small table in the middle of the restaurant and I laughed so, so much. We talked about our insecurities and neuroses and his first date with Lena Dunham and first-date vomiting in the bathroom and my hopes for my record and how much we love Tegan and Sara and how weird the music industry is and on and on. We managed to skip over all the politeness and chitchat, something I seem to have become more allergic to as I have gotten older. We agreed a writing session would indeed be fun. We made arrangements for a time to meet up back in NYC, when he had a little time off. During our month of e-mailing I had wondered if I would fall in love with Jack (because I think that about every new man I meet). I did fall for him, but as a friend from the very beginning, which made everything moving forward delightfully uncomplicated and easy.

As you might recall, cowriting is not my favorite experience. Despite how much I liked Jack, I was playing out how horrible it all might go in my mind as I went up the ten or so floors to a little writing room in a big studio in Times Square. I was the first to arrive. I unpacked my computer and a notebook and tried to figure out what you are supposed to do when you are the first one to arrive at a writing session. There was a huge recording console that I couldn't even pretend to know how to use, some massive speakers I couldn't figure out how to turn on, and a mute little keyboard that was connected to all of it. I poked around the adjacent lounge for a minute, very disappointed *not* to find a coffee machine anywhere, which would have been a task that I was pretty sure I could stretch into taking up at least ten minutes. I was flooded with relief when Jack came fumbling in with his backpack and lightning-fast conversation and a couple of crinkly bags from a pharmacy where he goes frequently because, he told me with a smile, he's a self-diagnosed hypochondriac. I began to relax.

We chatted a little bit as the studio tech helped get everything up and running. Jack was in the midst of a world tour with his band, FUN., and selling out arenas all over the globe, writing songs with loads of different artists *and* for his new project, Bleachers, falling in love with Lena, and he somehow seemed completely in control of and energized by all of it. In addition, Jack was consumed with the launch of the Ally Coalition, his social justice organization built around inviting straight voices to speak out for gay rights. Marriage equality was all over the news, and we talked about how, state by state, we were watching history unfold. It was a very exciting time.

I told him about a past trip to New York where I realized how much more I wanted from my life. I was at a personal crossroads and change was nagging at me. I had just made the decision to leave Los Angeles, and also to strike out on a new creative path with this record. I was contemplating making changes having to do with my long-term band mates, and I hadn't had the courage to talk about it with them yet. I was also considering embarking on my very first solo tour, but wasn't sure if I could pull it off. Thankfully, this was easy to divulge to Jack, who, with his unapologetic honesty, can always somehow one-up your worries in a way that is both hilarious and utterly charming.

He makes me laugh, which makes me relax, which makes room for music.

This meeting came at a time when I was feeling pressure to get the new record done quickly, but was very stuck in my own writing. We jumped into Jack's catalogue and listened to unfinished demo ideas from his computer. He scrolled through a catalogue of song seeds and we stopped because one of them grabbed me. It ended up being the genesis of Brave. The rolling drum loop began, and then a sound that felt like a starting-line gunshot signaled the plinking piano to begin its familiar chord progression at the top of the verse. It felt like some song I had known before and was now just trying to remember. The immediate connection made me want to create, and we spent the next couple of hours going over rhythmic ideas for the verses, homing in on a melody.

It was then that Jack gave me a gift I didn't know I needed.

"You don't need help writing lyrics," he said, and basically sent me out of the room. I was a little stunned. Over the years I had made an erroneous assumption that cowriting had to look a certain way, where everything was shared, including the lyrics. I had always tried to be uncompromisingly inclusive of my cowriters through each step of the writing, and mostly I would come away feeling like something got diluted along the way. I feel silly admitting it now, but it had never actually occurred to me that it was okay to simply tell a story by myself while still collaborating. Hunting for the exact words that communicate my thoughts in a song is my greatest pleasure. My lyrics are my most private prayers, and I guess I don't really know how to authentically share that part of my craft. At least not yet. And Jack saw that before I did. He gently gave me permission to own the story of my songs without apology.

Thanks, Jack.

I sat in the lounge next to the studio and the words poured out ferocious and fast. Partially sparked by the idea behind Jack's advocacy organization, they became a love letter to a very dear friend of mine who was, as I was, facing big things at the time and feeling powerless and fearful. She was living between an internal and an external reality that didn't match. After many years of keeping her private life *very* private, she was struggling to come out with her evolving sexuality to friends and family and didn't yet see a way to do it. She shamed herself into believing that people wouldn't be able to love her as she truly was, and who she was becoming. I had watched her turmoil and anxiety grow over the years. They had become bigger and bigger beasts that made her believe she was small and weak. Stuck. From the outside I could see that those fears kept her from considering the very *possibility* that there might be a better version of her life waiting for her. It mirrored so many things in my life. I recognized all of it. Although the issues at the heart of my situation were different, both of our stories boiled down to the same thing: fear of speaking our truth.

My friend became the conduit for the message that I needed to hear myself. I spoke directly to her with my lyrics. I wrote to her about how we can choose to reflect the places we see the lack of love in the world, or we could try to be stronger than our weaknesses, and shine a light on something better. We were facing down our own personal Goliaths. I wanted to invite her to stand with me and try the radical act of simply staying put. To tell the truth and trust that whatever comes next is going to be okay.

Jack was moved by the message and gave me the sense that anything and everything is possible. That this song had the potential to deeply connect with a lot of people. I felt something inside of me expanding. I am a creature of habit, and I live most comfortably inside intimate writing. I write songs about the nuance and minutiae of the heart's condition, and when I imagine sharing those songs it feels like a conversation between my listeners and me. If I am a small theater with velvet seats, then Jack is a stadium with fireworks. This is another one of his very special qualities as a writer and collaborator. He has a talent for creating sweeping musical anthems effortlessly, broad and bright, and this doesn't mean he doesn't speak to what is intimate about the human condition; he just does it in a way that conjures up the feeling of a common purpose and oceans of people, lighters and all.

It was exciting to have an idea come this quickly; still, we left the studio that first day without a chorus. We felt that the verses were special, and we had played around with a few directions for what came next, but nothing felt right. At the end of the day, I went back to my hotel in SoHo and let things marinate. I decided I would go in early the next day to get some time alone with the keyboard and see if I could crack the code.

The next morning I walked through the bedlam of Times Square and had about an hour to myself before Jack arrived. I sat at the keyboard trying to condense the thoughts and feelings pinging around my head into its nucleus. My best friend's journey. My belief in her undeniable strength that she didn't see. The changing climate surrounding my friends in the gay community. Jack's advocacy group. My own journey toward another city and a new life. My hope for my own ability to keep going. It all seemed to boil down to a request for a simple intention.

It wasn't about prowess. Or outcome. My request was for courage. To turn and face the thing that scares you the most and do your best to stay there. I asked for honesty, which sometimes requires more strength than most things we do in our lives. I can put my hand over my heart and sing those words and mean them, every single time.

I want to see you be brave.

I felt chills when I sang them over the melodic hook that I had plunked out for the first time that day in the studio, the melody that also happened to be at the VERY, VERY top of my range. I was pleading for the strength to be courageous on behalf of my best friend, myself, and everyone I could imagine who needed it, and the request belonged at my vocal breaking point: a high E-flat. The break between my chest voice and head voice happens to occur on the first two notes of the hook of the song. Those two little notes have kicked my ass many times, and that song has taught me more about surrender and truth than I could have imagined.

Jack loved it. We finessed the structure and made a quick recording. I e-mailed our demo of the song off to my manager and it was the second song in my career that caused him to call me right after he heard it to tell me how special it was. We decided that Brave would be the first single from the upcoming record, which I was just about to start recording. I knew when the song was finished that we had made something that was undeniably honest, but it was also my most pop-oriented, commercial-sounding song up to this point. I wondered if that was going to come back to bite me.

Summer Shapiro and myself dancing like maniacs in downtown Los Angeles

The next few months went by unbelievably fast. I finished up the writing, began settling into my new home in New York City, and simultaneously started recording in both New York and LA with two different producers. I wanted to explore a range of stylistic approaches, and each producer brought something special and unique to the recording process. I coproduced most of the record at Electric Lady Studios with John O'Mahony and Kurt Uenala, and it was exhilarating and easy. We did almost everything by ourselves, drank red wine, ate vegan meals followed by non-vegan chocolate, and invited

friends to play on the recordings. The music unfolded before us
as something exploratory and exciting. Anxiety bled into excitement that told me I was making something that would commem-
orate the personal transformation I was experiencing in my life.
At some point during those months, I received an e-mail from a
friend with a quote in it. It gave me the title of the record.

> *"There is a vitality, a life force, an energy, a quickening*
> *that is translated through you into action, and because there*
> *is only one of you in all of time, this expression is unique.*
> *And if you block it, it will never exist through any other*
> *medium, and it will be lost. The world will not have it.*
>
> *It is not your business to determine how good it is, nor*
> *how valuable, nor how it compares with other expressions. It*
> *is your business to keep it yours clearly and directly, to keep*
> *the channel open. You do not even have to believe in yourself*
> *or your work. You have to keep yourself open and aware to*
> *the urges that motivate you. Keep the channel open.*
>
> *No artist is pleased. [There is] no satisfaction whatever*
> *at any time. There is only a queer, divine dissatisfaction, a*
> *blessed unrest that keeps us marching and makes us more*
> *alive than the others."*

—MARTHA GRAHAM, to Agnes de Mille

I would call the record *The Blessed Unrest*. I talked myself
into believing that even though I didn't know exactly where I
was going, the journey itself must be divinely ordained, lead-

ing me toward something better. The message of this quote seemed to seamlessly fit into the message of Brave and I was struck by a sense of synergy with how everything was coming together. I didn't have time to get my SYNERGY tattoo, however, because things that come together can also come apart.

I recorded the song Brave in Los Angeles with a producer named Mark Endert, who was given the few songs we intended to service to radio. Mark has a great ear for pop radio, and a killer résumé. He is kind and funny and has big ideas, amazing stories, and a bulldozer work ethic. He saw me struggle internally in the studio with my worry that the song was sounding too pop and too commercial. I have spent my whole career worrying that the big bad pop monster was going to eat me when I wasn't looking, and it speaks more to my stubborn streak than anything else, but that familiar fear was there in my stomach, gnawing away. I wrestled with myself to reserve judgment until I heard the finished product. I struggled to make something meaningful to me and still gently shape it for what we hoped would be a life on the radio. I was very emotional during the recording, feeling like I was being invisibly bullied—by whom, I'm not sure— but I gave a lot of space for his ideas and we made something together that was very rhythmic and bright and pretty perfect for radio. He added a lot of programming at his studio in Florida and sent me the initial mix of what we had done together.

I absolutely hated it.

It was slick and shiny and I felt that I had lost my hold on the essence of the song. Like I had "sold out" to get my song on the radio. Nothing makes me more panicky and rage-filled than the worry that I've done something in order to position myself for business over the art. (And yes, my label and management LOOOOVE that side of me.) I sat in my car listening over and over again, afraid that I had contaminated something that could have been pure. We were running out of time to get the single on its way, and I made the decision to take my own advice. I talked honestly to Mark about it, and although he didn't hear quite what I was hearing, we agreed to make some adjustments and had another session to try and get on the same page. I walked into that session ready to hate everything including Mark, and feeling absolutely certain the whole song was going to need to be completely rerecorded.

We started by simply hearing everything that was there, piece by piece. The programming. The string parts. The synthesizers. The background vocals. The live drums. Bass. Guitar. I sat with my arms crossed and my temples throbbing with anger and begrudgingly realized I *really* liked 90 percent of what was there. It was beautiful. Slick, absolutely, but also bold and hopeful. It was leaning into that shiny pop place that I always fight against but secretly really love, and this song wore it well. We did decide to strip some of it away to leave a little more space, and then Mark made some sonic adjustments to accommodate something slightly more natural. The heart of it stayed very much the same, and the song settled into where it is now. I had been so afraid that my essence would get lost in all the bells and whistles that I couldn't allow myself to think that it might also feel authentic to have a song that sounded like that.

After we had made our changes, I wanted to double-check my own instincts by doing what I *never* do—I asked for opinions. From my family. My friends. My management. Jack. I cringed listening along with them, waiting for them to hear something fake or paper-thin, but every single one of them loved it. I started to listen without fighting back, and began to hear what they heard. I'd asked for honesty and I got it. They heard a pop song with heart. I smiled internally and realized that this was going to be a really special song in my life.

JACK ANTONOFF

I was having dinner with Mike Birbiglia and Sara Quin, and the two of them were really getting intense about how much I would love Sara Bareilles. They were really going in hard about her. Sometime after that dinner, Sara Quin put us in touch over e-mail and we kind of hit the ground running.

I remember one specific e-mail from Sara B that was nearly three thousand words, separated into small paragraphs chronologically outlining her day from four a.m. to midnight. She went to the airport a day early and walked me through all the actual events and bizarre emotions that come along with getting yourself to LAX crazy-early the day before you were supposed to be there. I just loved her immediately.

We met in person at a small restaurant in West LA for breakfast. I don't remember the exact time, but it was during

/ *Jack Antonoff and I in New York City, May 2015*

this specific period when FUN. was working at an insane
pace and I constantly felt like I couldn't breathe. When life
is crazy like that I always remember so little; everything is

fast and blurry, but meeting Sara that day existed outside of everything crazy. It was strange like that. I saw her and felt oddly comfortable immediately.

We talked about relationships, death, anxiety, strange career feelings, etc. We laughed a lot—I remember *actually* laughing. Sara was talking about a strange and transitional place she was in and I remember feeling very much there myself at the time. I had been doing a bunch of different production and writing sessions on my days off; some of them were so inspiring, some of them made me want to shoot myself.

I've always written songs in a very safe and lonely space, and working outside of that was terrifying for me. Two artists in a room creating something that is bigger than either one of them is incredibly beautiful. On the other side, working to create something with someone for an artist you don't know is repulsive. I was in the midst of what my comfort zone was for writing and production. The week before I went to the factory-farming equivalent session for a pop star I won't name. Sara and I discussed this. We talked about all the horrible and wonderful things that can come from stepping outside of your writing comfort zone. Knowing it could be a disaster, we said we'd try it.

I made a beat called Frankie at my parents' house in New Jersey a few days before we went into the studio together. I was living at my parents' house at the time and I'd just work on anything that came into my head whenever I was home. A lot of these ideas would become the Bleachers album, but rarely there would be these other ideas that I would be so in love with but couldn't create a song out of. The beat and chords for this Frankie thing was exactly that (I don't know why it was called Frankie). It felt different, like it had this rolling quality that made me want to listen on a loop. I remember thinking, "Fuck, if that beat feels that good, imagine a great song on it," but I couldn't write anything. Somehow, it didn't feel like me.

I put Frankie in a special folder on my iTunes labeled "Really Good," which exists separately from my "Writing" folder, which at the time was also separate from the "Bleachers" and "FUN." folders. Everything got dumped into the "Writing" folder, and then very few things would end up in "Really Good" that didn't just go to "Bleachers" or "FUN."

Sara seemed somewhat nervous when we first started working. I was, too. There is always this feeling at the beginning of a session with someone you've never worked with before where you just don't know if anything is going to be possible. It's a strange feeling, it's the opposite of cozy. We talked for a while and I played her some stuff I was working on. A song I did with Tegan and Sara, some random demo stuff, and then I started playing her different track and chord ideas. I was running her through different ideas in the "Really Good" folder and she stopped me when she heard Frankie. From that point everything was simple.

As it was happening, Brave was the easiest and most joyous song I've ever been a part of. There were no moments I remember struggling over a part. Sara's lyrics seem to spill out of her. Each layer we added I could feel the song coming more and more alive. There is actually almost no part of Brave that we wrote or demoed that isn't exactly what it ended up being. That is so rare. The best songs are the ones that just come out. Nothing felt forced because Sara was actually writing lyrics that were especially inspiring in that moment—to her personally, to me after conversations we had been having that day in the studio, and to the world, given that moment in history with the fight for LGBTQ rights. The parts were the same way. They flowed out. Sara's moving bass parts on the piano of the chorus dictated the beat in that part; the triumphant lyrics gave total license for the drums to be super bombastic.

I didn't have much perspective on it. The day after that New York session I flew to London. I remember editing vocals and working it out on the plane. I showed it to some of the guys in FUN.; they gave me this feeling that it was something really next level. I remember sending it to my publisher, who called me freaking out about what was then labeled I Wanna See You Be Brave.

Its funny like that—you don't understand something when it's easy. Like falling in love with someone—just kind of happens without making any real effort or big plans. Important songs come out that way as well. When I hear Brave or hear a beautiful story from someone who it's meant a great deal to, it just makes me think of spending time with Sara. It just makes me think of having breakfast with her, getting to know her, laughing about how absurd our work can be, having intense conversations about politics and human rights—basically just her and I hanging out.

As time goes on and I write more and more, it's so clear to me that being in that free space is the only way to create something with weight. Working with Sara those days has shaped my outlook on writing more than I can express.

———

The song got released in April 2014, and I braced myself for the inevitable frenzy that would come when it shot to number one on every chart in the world. I was sure this song was going to connect with the masses with the same kind of explosive energy I had felt when we wrote it. I wrote in my journal about how difficult it was going to be to handle the amount of attention the song would get. I tried to emotionally prepare myself for rising to a new level of fame and what would come with that. I finally understood how Oprah must feel.

Cue humble pie. The song didn't "shoot" in any direction at all; although Brave was warmly received and definitely supported on the radio, there was no fanfare. Not even a parade in my honor. It was just another song out in the world. It's embarrassing that I let my ego have so much real estate, but again I was reminded there is always room for more humility. It's one thing to dream of connecting in a big way; it's another thing to crave attention. I tucked my tail between my legs and practiced my gratitude for what was in front of me: preparing for my first solo tour in May, which was *terrifying*. I called it the Brave Enough tour to acknowledge that I was facing a long-held fear of mine of playing solo shows. I was brave enough to try and do something that truly scared me, but in the midst of my preparation for the tour I encountered an entirely new issue:

I couldn't sing the fucking song live.

It was too high. I'd known it was at the top of my range when we recorded it in the studio, but you can sing it as many times as you need to get a good performance, so I didn't think much of it. Take dinner breaks. Try it on different days. Drink bourbon. You are bound to hit the notes at least a few times and bim bam boom, you got a song. But *sustaining* the practice of singing a song like this was new territory. I would have to sing it multiple times a day, at eight in the morning for radio promo, at sound-check parties, and every night on tour. I would have to sing it on TV eventually, and there I was in the rehearsal room and it felt like there was only a 50/50 chance for me to hit those notes or not. I panicked and paced and sang until my throat hurt. I eventually asked for help, and with the guidance of a wonderful voice coach named Wendy Parr, we broke it down. I bawled like a baby in our coaching session, sharing how limited I felt in my own abilities. Now the song represented all my fear in a whole new way. I felt like a fraud, and thank God there had been no parades in my honor. I'm a hack.

Wendy guided me to softening and staying put. She made me walk around the room stomping through imaginary rain puddles to get me back in my body, and then she helped me find the placement for these notes in my mouth and throat. She subtly sculpted some of my vowel sounds on the high notes, and then after not too long, I actually got it. It was clear it would take work to get comfortable, but I saw it begin to become possible. The whole thing was about trust and facing difficulty, and the irony was fucking thick as molasses. The song was here yet again to teach me about humility and hot damn: message received.

I went on my tour and learned that I was capable of putting on a solo show, communing with my fans in an entirely new way that made me light up. I stretched into new territory, and all the while, Brave was out there in the world, making its own connections. This song took on a dynamic life of its own over the next year, and I started seeing the effect it was having on *people*, not on the charts. During my solo tour, we launched an art project where fans were asked to fill in the blank on a square card: I Am Brave Enough to _____. The cards ended up on Instagram under the hashtag #IAmBraveEnough.

The answers were astounding:

Donate bone marrow.

Go to nursing school.

Wear glasses.

Come out to my family.

Admit that I need help and to seek it.

Speak out against my abusive father.

Attend a concert in DC by myself and make new friends.

Beat cancer.

Stop letting doubt consume my life.

Fight our infertility.

Share my brain injury story.

The list goes on and on and on. I was leveled by the courage of total strangers to be vulnerable, and felt like this song

On a rooftop in Chelsea,
New York City, March 2013

was the greatest gift I had ever received. I felt closer to and more inspired by humans than ever. Late one night I was sent a link to a video made by the University of Minnesota Masonic Children's Hospital. A bald little boy in a Superman cape ran out the doors of the hospital as my song played in the background, and dozens of nurses and doctors and children danced around playfully, singing the words of Brave, inspiring each other to stay positive in the face of hardship. I wept. Over a million people would eventually see this video. It ended up on CNN and on news outlets all over the country. Many more videos and stories like this would spring up. Brave had become an anthem of sorts, and I felt like the song was a part of a little mini movement. I couldn't have been more proud.

Pema Chödrön is one of my favorite spiritual teachers. In her book *The Places That Scare You* she writes,

"The essence of bravery is being without self-deception."

I have spent so much time and energy in my life telling myself hundreds of little lies. Lies about the way I feel or don't feel. Lies about what I want. Lies about the things I want to do. Lies about the people who make me feel safe or the kind of art I actually want to make. All these lies that muddy up the honest conversation I could have been having with myself and the world around me.

I don't know who I thought I was helping.

Who am I when I am stripped of all of that? Who am I if I build my life on my deepest, most soul-crushing truth? Who stays with me? Who disappears? What happens if I feel pain but don't run from it and instead learn to feel it? Or if I feel vulnerable and don't hide it? If I feel ignored and ridiculed and don't pretend it doesn't hurt? What would happen if I found a way to speak up honestly as often as I possibly could? If I was just brave enough to try?

Well, I'm working on it.

I wrote my friend a letter when I first started writing this chapter for the book, to thank her—officially—for being my muse. It occurred to me that I might not have been explicit in letting her know how much she was a part of the story. She had already come out to her family months prior to this note and is still, every day, stepping bravely and truthfully into the light. She is stunning.

SHE

used to

BE
MINE

She Used to Be mine

It's not simple to say
That most days I don't recognize me
That these shoes and this apron
That place and its patrons
have taken more than I gave them
  It's not easy to know I'm not anything
like I used to be although it's true
I was never attention's sweet center
  I still remember that girl
She's imperfect but she tries
She is good, but she lies
She is hard on herself
She is broken but won't ask for help
She is messy, but she's kind
She is lonely most of the time
She is all of this mixed up and
  baked in a beautiful pie
  She is gone, but she used to be mine.

SHE USED TO BE MINE

SHE USED TO BE MINE was the first song I wrote for my musical. That, by the way, is a really fun sentence to type.

For years now, I have been fantasizing about how I would dive back into the world of the music I grew up on, the music of musical theater. As a child, I was captivated by the scores of shows like *The Sound of Music*, *Oklahoma!*, and *Evita*. *A Chorus Line*, *Les Misérables*, *The Phantom of the Opera*, *West Side Story*, *Annie*, and *The Scarlet Pimpernel*. *Miss Saigon*, *The*

Secret Garden, Tommy, Chess, The Mystery of Edwin Drood, Little Shop of Horrors . . . and many, many more. I developed a way of listening to music because of those shows, and because of that, I learned a particular way of writing that would show up down the line. The focus was acutely on the storytelling, bringing the audience along on a character's journey, sharing their emotional evolution, all delivered with some unforgettable melodies. I experienced the power of deepening a dramatic moment with a song. I also learned that I was not a true soprano, no matter how hard I clenched my butt cheeks. I tried to sing the part of Christine in *The Phantom of the Opera* dozens of times, melodramatically staring myself down in my nightgown in my bedroom mirror, and tragically falling short of the high E she sings at the end of the title song until I actually gave myself a headache one time and had to sit down for a few minutes. In spite of my injuries, the seeds were sown deep and true, and my love for the genre has never faded.

I have gotten farther and farther away from traditional theater in my career, but always held on to a hope that someday I would find my way back. Never in a million years did I imagine that would be because I wrote a musical that would be headed to the Great White Way (which is NOT the name of a shark highway but a nickname for Broadway, which I did not know until about six months ago). It's a fantastic turn of events, and I have a country music star to thank for a big part of it.

Jennifer Nettles and I were acquaintances, but became friends when I spent the summer opening for her band, Sugarland. This was an enormous tour. Eight buses, twelve semitrucks, and an elaborate two-story stage configuration that all centered around Jennifer and her musical partner, Kristian Bush. In all my years of touring, this was the first time I had opened for a band that had a female out front, and I studied her like a textbook, both on- and offstage. Onstage, I noticed how she was able to command more space than I ever had. It was little things, like reaching her arms out to their full extension when she gestured, or speaking a little slower, more deliberately, so everyone in the crowd could understand. She held space and time for applause. She was undeniably in control. Offstage she was gracious and kind to the many folks on tour but kept deliberate boundaries that were not to be crossed. She commanded respect and consideration to preserve her energy for the stage, and I found it fascinating. She was a Star with a capital *S*.

There were lessons I took with me that I wish I had learned earlier in my career, like knowing what you want and not being afraid to ask for it. This can mean privacy, or fried chicken, whatever it is your soul is asking for. I also learned a respect for my own boundaries, because I saw how diligent Jennifer was with hers. Asking for what you need with kindness is a great skill, and doesn't mean you will always receive it, but it will certainly up your odds.

One day on tour, we sat down together on a grassy lawn outside a southern venue and I learned that we shared a love for musical theater and had both been harboring little-girl fantasies of starring on Broadway someday. Of course Jennifer, always the big thinker, immediately said, as if it was the most obvious way forward, "We should write a musical and star in it!!!" I laughed, thinking that it sounded like a crazy idea and, like most awesome crazy ideas, it would be forgotten the next day. You know, like New Year's resolutions, and remembering people's birthdays. I forgot that Jennifer has too much fire for a fade-out. She is a meticulous doer, and within a week, we had writing sessions scheduled into the tour and we developed the basic brushstrokes of a musical called *LESBIANS!*, about a women's college in the '90s. *LESBIANS!* didn't totally crystallize but was a pretty ambitious start for a couple of folks with no experience writing musicals. Over the next year we wrote a handful of songs, but the idea unraveled as we both got busier with touring, life, family, and other projects. We had a great time fantasizing, though. I never would have taken it seriously if not for her. It taught me to think bigger, and to get clear on what I want. Theater didn't have to be some nebulous pipe dream, but a real place that I could start aiming toward, and the whole process greased the wheels for what was coming. I have Jennifer's chutzpah to thank for that.

Side note: a couple of years after our adventure, her chutzpah also landed her a starring role as Roxy Hart in *Chicago* on Broadway. She was fabulous, and will most definitely be back for more. Love you, sis.

I started building a relationship with the theater in a real way, and formed new business relationships to help move me in that direction. In January of 2012, I took a trip to New York for both business and pleasure, and had my first meeting with Jack Tantleff, my brand-new theatrical agent. I arrived for brunch feverish and hungover (after a night that fell in the "pleasure" category) and spent a good portion of the meeting trying not to vomit in my bowl of tortellini in brodo. We talked about ways I could dip my toes in the Broadway world, and Jack had lots of great ideas, making it seem not only possible but plausible. I felt the butterflies in my stomach start churning as he talked about the different ways I could be involved. He mentioned a production of Stephen Sondheim's *Into the Woods* that would be going up in Central Park the following summer, and that I might be right for the role of Cinderella. The timing would be perfect: I was in between record cycles. It would also give me an actual reason to spend a big chunk of time in New York City besides just "I want to go to there." My toes tingled, I was beyond excited.

My team set up the audition and I felt fancy and entitled and cocky and returned to New York a few weeks later to promptly get my ass handed to me. In a high-rise rehearsal room studio in midtown, in my casual sweater set, I basically one-arm army-crawled through that audition. I was underprepared and under-qualified. My heart raced and my voice shook as I wobble-sang Sondheim and overacted the shit outta my lines in the scenes. We all could simultaneously see that there was no way in hell I was going to pull off that role, but the creative team was so kind. As they ushered me out, I didn't even hear a snicker as the door closed behind me. The experience was humiliating and unforgettable—an extremely important lesson in respect. I knew that I had a ton of work to do if I ever hoped to step on a Broadway stage.

A couple of months passed and I received a phone call from Jack saying that there was a woman who wanted to have lunch and talk about the prospect of working together. A team of people were working on the stage adaptation of a film I hadn't seen yet, a film called *Waitress*, which had come out in 2007, an instant indie classic. I was enticed by the idea of getting involved with a show at its earliest stages, and curious about what they were looking for in me. I agreed to have a lunch meeting with the director, Diane, to get more information on what this whole project entailed. I guess I could imagine myself as a waitress. . . .

I didn't know who Diane Paulus was when I sat down with her a Times Square restaurant: old school, with white tablecloths and an elderly lunch crowd. She wore all black and no makeup, dark hair falling below her shoulders, her shiny hazel eyes tucked under wild eyebrows. I liked her immediately. She is direct and articulate, curious and intelligent. I didn't know then that she is one of the most sought-after visionaries and highly regarded directors working in the theater community, or that she would be named among *Time* magazine's one hundred most influential people in the world. I didn't know she had won multiple Tony Awards and was creative director of the American Repertory Theater at Harvard, one of the foremost incubators for groundbreaking theater projects. I just sat there in my not knowing, and ordered soup and salad thinking *I* was supposed to be wooed. Ugh. Kill me.

Our conversation meandered through our lives starting with our childhoods—she in New York City, coolly walking

/ Diane Paulus

past drug dealers at ten years old, and me in the forest, my
blonde pony, Muffin, bucking me off over her bitch-face little
head. It was nice to have so much in common from the get-go.
Diane asked me if I had ever considered writing for a musical.
Of course I'd played around with the idea with Jennifer, but at
the time we were a couple of friends exploring an idea, dipping
toes in what felt like frivolous and playful waters. This was
official. A big Broadway director was asking me to take on the
responsibility for building a musical world, just like the ones
I grew up on. It sounded huge and quite impossible. It wasn't
that I thought of myself as someone who never *would* write a

musical; I honestly thought I was someone who never *could.* Her unwavering belief in my potential was flattering to say the least, and I wondered if I could trust her confidence in me. I considered the idea seriously. Could I do that? Could I do that amazing thing? I had no idea.

Diane Paulus casts pretty incredible spells. Her slight-framed gravitas pushes the boundaries around what you think is possible with just a few short sentences. Familiar "limitations" become just bendy ol' suggested guidelines that get reexamined and potentially redefined. All of this is coupled with a dead-serious intent of delivering something special and an obsessive work ethic that doesn't have time for anything but everyone's best. It's like, "Ha-ha, yeah I know it's *impossible* to make the stage disappear, but ha-ha-ha, no, no, seriously, do it and call me when it's done." It's powerful to be around someone who sees great potential where you might not. I felt an invitation to join her in an experiment, so I agreed. I told her I would go watch the film, and that if there was a spark, I guessed I would try to write a musical. And that was that.

I watched the film by myself in my one-bedroom West Village apartment. It follows Jenna, played by Keri Russell, who finds herself in a loveless marriage and an unfulfilled life. She is plain in many ways but gifted with a talent for baking pies: she escapes her ordinary surroundings with strange and unusual recipes that both reflect her most soulful self and nourish the community around her. When she finds out she has accidentally gotten pregnant by her abusive husband, she immediately turns her attention to how she might escape everything for good. Her journey involves lots of pie, good friends, Andy Griffith, gynecological sex, depression, and learning to love in the biggest way possible. I felt like I could sink my teeth in to this character, and her story felt personal to me (besides the gynecological sex). She is broken, very flawed, very human, and I loved her immediately.

I officially joined the project, guided through the process by the rest of the mostly female creative team, which also felt exciting to me, as I'm very often the only woman in the room when it comes to business. We had our first creative meeting around a conference table in an office building in Manhattan, eating stale pastries over blank yellow legal pads. We all watched the movie together and paused at certain moments, to discuss character, structure, backstory, motivation, potential song placement, and questions that needed answering about the plot. People said new and exciting phrases like "dramaturgical issues." I was euphoric. Even in its very first stages, collaborating on this project felt like a puzzle to solve, and I was responsible for my little corner, but it was only a portion of the greater finished product. My job was all about making the characters as rich and three-dimensional as possible with song and to think outside the box in order to do so. The process reminded me of writing music before I had any experience with the business. Unfettered. Playful. Instinctual.

I went home with a very rough idea of how to get started. It was about reacting to and capturing what felt the most immediate from the characters. There were moments in the film that emotionally swelled, and I could see how the experience

Nadia DiGiallonardo, music director, and me

might be deepened with a song. With my natural penchant for melancholy, I rewatched the scene that depicts Jenna's darkest, most broken place. She is very pregnant, and has saved almost enough money to leave her husband when he finds her stash and wildly falls apart at her feet. His rage is actually his fear of being abandoned and he clings to her like a child. She has the choice to continue toward leaving, or sink back into staying. She decides to surrender to him. It's absolutely heartbreaking. I was struck by what kept her in place, her fear of hurting him. It reminded me of my own darkest moments, waking up one day, looking around, and not recognizing your own self, because you have given too much of that away.

Jenna's song would begin just after this scene.

I wanted the song to be simple. Feminine. Melancholy. The melody needed to feel a little bit like a lullaby, an homage to her growing baby as Jenna attempts to soothe herself in this painful moment. I implemented lots of repetition of phrase to show her stuckness, but also her breaking point. I wanted her voice to be at its breaking point too, but only for a moment. Jenna is reclaiming herself in this song, calling out her circumstance by name for the first time but, sadly, without a resolution. She is talking about the person she used to be and how far away she feels from her, panicked that there is no way to get her back. I cried when I wrote it. I still cry when I hear it. It's my song too.

I began to build the score. I was chipping away at what felt like an impossibly tall order, but little by little it started to take shape. Some songs appeared more easily than others, and some should have never appeared at all. I wrote a song that will never again see the light of day, about Jenna's husband, Earl, trying to have sex with her. I couldn't think of anything creative to say with that moment, so I just had him spell out the letters of the phrase:

P-L-E-A-S-E-H-A-V-E-S-E-X-W-I-T-H-M-E.

Like, I made him *sing* that. Spelling it out. Over and over. We were preparing for a staged reading and we went through the script with the actors who were stepping into these roles for that week. Diane turned to me and said, "Okay. What exactly is this song?"

I didn't have a good answer, which, for everyone reading this, is *always* answer enough, but we were too close to the performance to pull the plug. Our associate director had the idea to at least give the character a little comic relief by adding two dancing sperm to sing the background vocals. When dancing sperm save you, you are in trouble. During that scene at the reading, I wanted to crawl under my chair and pretend I had nothing to do with that song, but instead I quietly sat there watching the dancing sperm and said to myself, *Rewrite.*

I'm sure Rodgers and Hammerstein made similar mistakes, right?*

This was all a positive progression, however, because I became less precious about my ideas. Some of them were terrible, clearly, but I worked on simply putting pen to paper and, more important, opening up for feedback. I had experiences where I thought I was moved by a musical idea, but realized in sharing that I wasn't pushing myself. I wrote a song for the Andy Griffith character, Joe, that was a sweet tune but a generic rip-off of a cliché "musical theater" song. It was at best an acceptable placeholder: inoffensive but unremarkable. My soul mate—friend, collaborator, and scriptwriter Jessie Nelson reminded me that this show would be my opportunity to give

---

* No, they didn't.

the audience something only I could give. It was the kindest way for her to tell me "You can do better." And she was right. I dug deeper and deeper and poured so much of myself into the score that I know even though it won't be perfect by any stretch of the imagination, there is nothing in there that doesn't have a ton of heart. That much I know for sure.

Casting the right leading lady was crucial. The character of Jenna had become beloved to me, my talisman for renewal. I knew I didn't have the acting skills yet to bring her to life, but handing her over to someone else felt scary. Deep into our creative process, amidst our many, many meetings about writing and rewriting and casting and schedule, I went to see the opening night of Carole King's musical, *Beautiful*. In the past year of my life, Carole had become my unofficial guru and guided me through some very tough moments. I first met her in Cleveland as I stood side stage at the 2012 Rock and Roll Hall of Fame induction ceremony, shaking uncontrollably, waiting to perform a song to honor the late, great Laura Nyro. I had nothing but nerves and panic and fear, and Carole simply put her hand on my back and said, "Relax. Everyone is going to love you! Just get out of your own way." It was so simple, and so loving. The two of us shared the stage at the 2014 Grammy Awards, our pianos facing each other, smiling and singing a medley of her song Beautiful and my song Brave. It was a cornerstone moment in my career. A day later, she was one of the first people to call me after the very painful event when I fired my manager of ten years. In her gentle yet firm way, she reminded me that I am a strong and capable

/ Jessie Mueller and I at ART workshop rehearsal

person who can do anything in this world and that above all I am loved. Carole's place in music history is untouchable, built upon craft and talent and grace, and she has become my lighthouse in the industry. Knowing her as a person makes it all that much easier to celebrate her accomplishments, and I was deeply emotional watching the brand-new musical about her life. A young actress named Jessie Mueller played Carole, and she was riveting. I couldn't take my eyes off her. She told Carole's incredible story with an earthy grace that was so pure and so grounded . . . so true to who Carole is in the world. And her voice is transcendent. I hugged Jessie after the show and thanked her for her gifts.

I knew exactly who I wanted to give Jenna to.

Incidentally, I had a good laugh recently when I learned who got the part of Cinderella in that Central Park production of *Into the Woods* instead of me.

It was Jessie. Well, she also accepted the part of Jenna. I couldn't have been happier.

Full circle, beeyotches.

When we got word that Jessie would be moving on from the show in March 2017, I felt a lot of things. First, gratitude for her craftsmanship and dedication to the storytelling on behalf of our lead character, Jenna Hunterson. Jessie was remarkable, and audiences adored her.

Second, I felt a small spark ignite: Maybe I could continue the legacy of this role that I had fallen in love with? I craved an opportunity to revisit my roots as a musical theater performer for the first time since high school. A lot of years have passed since my Audrey (spoiler alert) got eaten by the plant in *Little Shop of Horrors*, but I still had the itch to step onstage again. The stars had aligned.

I thought I knew the show intimately, but discovering my Jenna was entirely new. I met with acting coaches. I bought books about pie. I played with baking utensils in my kitchen and laughed out loud at how ridiculous I felt.

Mostly, I worried I had bitten off more than I could chew.

But thanks to a month of rehearsals and guidance from the director Diane Paulus, the book writer Jessie Nelson, and the choreographer Lorin Latarro, I actually forgot to be scared sometimes.

My "opening night" was Friday, March 31. I felt sick to my stomach from the second I opened my eyes that morning, but it wasn't the familiar queasiness of too little sleep, or too much bourbon the night before. This was more like me as a child on Christmas morning, holding my breath as I unwrapped the box to reveal either the off-brand Cabbage Patch Kid, or the real one.

At two p.m., we had our final rehearsal—a full run-through of the show, without an audience. My voice and my hands were shaking; I barely remember speaking and singing the lines. What I do remember are strange little details, like how dry my mouth was through the opening number, and how the stage felt under my bare feet in my first scene at the doctor's office. I forgot my blocking entirely in one scene, broke character, and started laughing, then quickly remembered that this was the last time I could acknowledge a mistake to the audience.

I felt numb, but relieved that I got through the run-through at all.

The hours between the rehearsal and the show were a blur. A stream of flowers and gifts arrived to my dressing room, which came to look like either a flower shop or a funeral parlor. (Let's go with flower shop.) I had a notes session and a hug with Diane, and a shot of bourbon by myself. At seven thirty p.m. my hair was set in pin curls to prepare for my wig. Jenna's brunette ponytail was placed on my head. It all suddenly felt very real.

At 7:58 p.m. came the call for places. My dresser, Fran, arrived to help with my costume. I felt strangely calm. I walked down the stairs to the stage, where the cast was milling around, giving hugs and high fives. A frenetic buzzing energy in the building came from the audience and bled through the curtain onto us. We gathered at the center of the stage and put our hands in a pile to do a preshow cheer. We went to our places.

The lights went out and I looked down at my bright white sneakers in the dark behind the curtain I had seen so many times from the other side. It lifted and there was a wall of sound that I don't think I'll ever forget—a wild roar of sweet willingness to go on this ride with us.

The ride would last a couple of hours for the audience, but it was so much more than that to me.

The ride was four years of writing and rewriting lyrics and melodies, trying to pinpoint the sincerity and honesty in my contributions to the story.

Four years of watching it all come to life in conference rooms and living rooms and rehearsal rooms and workshops and an out-of-town theater and then, finally, a Broadway stage.

Four years of surrendering myself to this show wholeheartedly because I just couldn't figure out any other way to be alive.

I felt excitement, dread, gratitude, privilege, humility. For the next two-plus hours, I floated. Anticipation had worn out its welcome; it was simply time to unwrap the gift.

Joining the team of *Waitress* has turned out to be one of the best decisions I have ever made. The people who have come into my life because of it are some of nearest and dearest to my heart. The opportunity to observe and serve the vibrant and visceral world of theater has unbound my perception of what is possible. Being a part of this new community has revived my excitement for performance and the stage. And stretching my own artistic undertakings has made me look at myself differently. The songs born of this show are some of the proudest achievements of my whole career and they renewed something that I didn't know was withering away. They reminded me of what creating from a pure place feels like, and how joyful my work can be. Every time I take a train to Times Square, I'm like a little kid going to a playground, and it hasn't worn off yet. Broadway is a big business, and a honeymoon period can only last so long, but good God, I am holding on to it with all my might. I feel uplifted and full of possibility, reminded of the artist I was when I was writing music for the very first time. This feeling can be fleeting, so I am focused whole-heartedly on cherishing every moment of it while it lasts.

I think back to when I was a little girl, dreaming of stepping on the stage of a great theater someday. The seed that was planted back then as a child has been dormant but patient, and it is with hopeful eyes I watch it take root and rise up.

Dear Sara,

You just took a flight across the world to Barcelona, where you will spend the next six days trying to regain some sense of feeling like you are in control of your own life. It's not altogether intuitive to fly to Spain for the 4th of July to find your own independence again, but maybe there's poetry in there somewhere.

Your sister is here with you and you are grateful for that. You're finding an ease and honesty in her company that is making you feel less alone, although it also feels like hiding in a safe little cave. Like the grown up you is facing a lot of stuff and the child just wants to hide and go play quietly in her big sister's room.

You finished your run as Jenna in *Waitress* close to three weeks ago now, and it launched you into a spiral of depression and anxiety that feel like old friends you haven't seen in a long time—ones you had hoped had just simply forgotten about you. They didn't. Hello, Darkness, My Old Friend, would be comforting to hear, but you don't like that song because it's too thorny and sad.

The first stop is your relationship and that scares you the most because it actually feels like the healthiest part of your life in a lot of ways. Joe's love for you is bigger than any you've ever known and he makes you feel cherished and seen. You are carrying so much guilt and self-loathing right now, it's hard to wear his love at all, but you're trying really hard. You hate feeling like you have to *try* to know how to receive love. He is offering you grace and patience and unconditional love and that doesn't look like it will change anytime soon. You're scared of it for some reason.

Both doing and leaving the show were exhausting, and you're reeling right now from the vacuum that its completion has created. It gave you way more than it took, but the taking was a deep and hollow kind of depletion that started slow and then was very swift and sure by the end. The physical fatigue and stress of doing it eight times a week has left you feeling empty and you don't know what you need to fill up again.

You were euphoric for so much of the run. Loved being inside the show. It was like stepping into a dollhouse you had helped build, and experiencing the magic of it all coming to life from the best seat in the house. You came to crave the ritual of the half-hour call because it gave you purpose. Adjusting the lighting in your dressing room, facing yourself in the mirror, and beginning some version of a transformation. Feeling the entire building doing the same thing. It was thrilling to be a part of something bigger than you, and to feel the show inside your bones, and watch it get easier. You learned to negotiate fatigue and not apologize for it. It was healing to wholeheartedly offer what was available of yourself to the audience, even if it wasn't perfect. You learned so much from the people around you. Something felt complete and whole.

But, as your character Jenna says, "everything changes." You have to turn toward the next project, and physically, emotionally, spiritually, you are raw. You're tired of this same scenario that seems to crop up every handful of months. The low that follows the high. You have so much ugliness inside you right now that it spills over when you look in the mirror, and you are hating your body again. It hasn't changed much, but you are in hypercritical mode and picking apart every little inch.

Your wrinkles are more pronounced and your skin is dry and your butt is bigger and your stomach feels full and soft. You're so bored of hearing yourself say these same words every few months. It makes you feel defeated, and like you are going to be stuck here in this feeling of hell forever.

You tell yourself that your next artistic project will be full of joy and excitement, but you don't know how to start, and the whole thing feels impossible. You feel pressure to write a record. You actually just realized in this moment that you WANT to write a record, but it feels stuck in your throat. The threadbare cloak of obligation to stay "productive" that you wear at all times is making you feel crazy and panicked. You know it's irrational but you worry that if you stop you will disappear.

You want to lie down somewhere soft and stay there forever.

———————

So here I am.

Somewhere soft.

I'm in the future. And I see you. You are beautiful.

I see you trying to use old tricks for new problems, because when something gets solved, you expect it to stay that way. You try the same solutions and then panic when they don't work. But this is like using old keys for new locks. We are in new territory. And let me tell you something . . . If you do this right, this life, *everything* will be new territory from here on out. So you can stop looking for mile markers you have already seen. They aren't here waiting for you, my love. You are forging ahead further into yourself, into this vast and wild terrain of your time here on earth, and even though you don't recognize the landscape you must take your own advice and be brave enough to keep going, because everything you want is tucked under the gentle folds of the unknown. What if you left open the possibility that your life will surprise and delight you?

You are moving into a deeper experience inside your own life. Your relationships are deepening. Your art is bigger. Your platform is expanding. YOU are expanding. Growth is hard and it hurts and it makes us feel like we have to cling to "solid" ground because it feels safe somehow. But you can't grow and stay the same all at once. It's time to shed some skin and that limiting belief that your professional productivity is what makes you valuable to the world.

I know you worry that if you stop you will disappear. Your voice will shrivel up. You will be forgotten. But this is a phantom fear. There is only one person in the world whose neglect can damage you. There is only one person who ever truly needs to remember who you really are. She is writing you a love letter right now.

So go ahead and wear out this old habit of getting small and nervous and wounded and tearful. You can feel shaken by how big the world is and how unfamiliar the experiences are. You can dance with doubting yourself for a minute, but then, my girl, stop pretending to believe what the goblins are saying and step into all of it with just the tiniest bit more humor... because you actually know that you are safe. You just don't see it yet.

Go, Sara. Enjoy this life. These opportunities. The gifts of feeling small. Make more music with it. Tell more stories. Let Joe love you. Love him back exactly as you can right now and trust that it will be enough. Let go of feeling like that part of your life has to look any particular way and believe him as he asks you to lean into the honesty and grace of letting someone see ALL of you. Becoming a partner is not a surrender of independence. Being true partners is the fireworks show. It is utterly groundbreaking for you, so lean in and be grateful that God sent you a true and beautiful heart who deeply loves you for yours.

Let go. Let go of all that does not serve you, and remember yourself. You already have the freedom you're seeking. Look up, and watch the display of fire and lights and smoke and oohs and aahs...

It's beautiful.

And so are you.

Love,
Sara

EPILOGUE

WITH THIS BOOK, I tried to share experiences in my life that helped me discover who I am. I shared a lot of things on these pages that are pretty private. My mom read a few of the essays and said they made her sad, as if she didn't know me as well as she thought she did. I understood what she meant, and took that as a great compliment, in a way, because it means I gave something to this book that I haven't given anywhere else. I didn't want to use this opportunity to give redundant information, or to write my own extended Wikipedia page. I wanted to make confessions and admissions in the hopes of watching myself surrender a little bit more than I have. I think I accomplished that and so I feel glad. And Mom, now you know that I've smoked weed. We can talk about it later.

I hope these essays have been comforting to someone reading it if for no other reason than to watch me openly admit *I have no idea what I'm doing*. I suspect most people feel that way, even if they don't fess up. Life is staggering, and all we can do is our best. My personal best seems the most accessible to me when I am being as honest as I can be. At this point in my life, I am attempting to make choices that move me toward what feels authentic, while saying yes to things that make my gut feel spooked with possibility. I have no idea what that means for my future, but for now, that means working on a musical. Releasing an album of musical theater songs. Building a one-woman show. Taking a meditation course. Trying to keep houseplants alive. You know, big things.

I want to say thank you for reading these snippets of my stories and songs. It meant a lot to be able to share them. More than I knew it would. I hope that there are many more to come, but unless hell freezes over, I won't be writing them down in another book.

That is, unless I do.

You are beautiful.

S

ACKNOWLEDGMENTS

THANK YOU.

To my fans, this is all for you, always.

Karyn Marcus, my editor and copilot through this odd and enchanted journey. You were steady and wise throughout this process, and your honesty encouraged mine. It actually made me love this book. Can you believe it? (Me neither!) Thank you.

Laura Nolan at Kuhn Projects, Jonathan Karp, Megan Hogan, and the entire Simon & Schuster team, I am so grateful for your belief in me and your willingness to take a chance on a first-time author. Laura Palese for a beautiful design. Shervin Lainez for beautiful pictures. Brandon Creed, Kevin Beisler, Alana Balden and all at the Creed Company, thank you for fielding frantic phone calls and encouraging me to continue when I wanted to jump ship. Doug Mark, Phil Sarna, Dvora Engelfield, Marty Diamond, and Larry Webman, thank you for making sense of what I'm doing (and always making it better). To my Sony ATV and Epic Records families, thank you for all the support, always.

To my friends and confidants for reading pieces from this book and telling me it was good enough to be a thing in the world. Jack Antonoff, Ben Folds, Sara Quin, Mona Tavakoli, Laura Jansen, Catherine Lacey, and Chris Morrissey. Thank you for your contributions to my book and to my life.

To my band and crew, past and present, thank you for your generosity in all ways. I have learned so much from you.

To Mom and Dad, my very first heroes, thank you for all the things you have taught me, and especially thank you for my sisters. You built a family that amazes me and challenges me every day. Thank you for encouraging me to always try and do my best, knowing I'll be loved no matter what. My whole family is pretty neat.

Thank you to Betty White for being, and the B-52s for Love Shack.

PHOTO CREDITS

———

Numbers refer to the pages on which the photos appear. All other photos are from the author's collection.

Courtesy of Sony Music Entertainment—Photograph taken by Autumn DeWilde: 64

Danny Clinch: 93, 159

Daniel Silbert: 26-27, 41, 129

Heidi Ross: 124-125

Jimmy Ryan Photography: 162-163, 172, 175, 179

Photo by Colin Young-Wolff: 5, 42-43, 57, 70-71, 114-115, 122

Travis Schneider: 134-135, 147

ABOUT THE AUTHOR

SARA BAREILLES is a seven-time Grammy Award–nominated, two-time Tony Award–nominated, and two-time Emmy Award–nominated singer, songwriter, and musician who has riveted millions of fans around the world with her warmly intimate voice, naturally melodic songs about heartache and resilience, and the spirited, anything-goes nature of her live performances. A self-taught pianist, the Eureka, California, native moved to Los Angeles at age eighteen and first broke through with her 2007 global number-one hit, Love Song. Her five albums have sold a collective 2.5 million copies and spawned such hits as King of Anything, Uncharted, and Brave, the latter from 2013's Album of the Year Grammy contender *The Blessed Unrest*. Her first full-length album since then, *Amidst the Chaos*, was released in 2019 to rave reviews, and between albums, Sara composed the music and lyrics for the hit Broadway musical *Waitress*. Known for her fearless candor and witty humor both onstage and off, Bareilles has employed her ample storytelling gifts to pen her first book, *Sounds Like Me*—a *New York Times* bestselling collection of essays told through the lens of the lyrics of some of her best-loved songs.